Dr. Tanya Skoro

THE SECRET OF

BULIMIA

**A new successful method
of overcoming the
incomprehensible pitfalls of
overeating**

**Discover the way to a healthy
figure without bulimic pain**

THE SECRET OF BULIMIA
by Dr. Tanya Skoro

Publisher
VANIS Ltd Pula

Translation from Croatian
LEKTOR d.o.o.
Jasenka Tezak Stefanic

English Editor
Alexander Douglas Hoyt

CIP – Publication classification
University Library in Pula
UDK   616.89-008.441.42
SKORO, Tanya
      The Secret of Bulimia: /
Tanya Skoro. – 3rd edition - Pula: Vanis, 2010
First published in 2009

ISBN 978-953-55505-1-8

IMPORTANT REMARK
As with all dietary plans and recommendations, when following the
dietary program presented in this book, continual and strict medical
monitoring and supervision by your physician is necessary once your
initial health condition has been precisely determined on the basis of
laboratory tests and specialist examinations.
This book is neither a medical manual nor a substitute for any therapy
prescribed by your physician.
The author and publisher hereby waive all liability pertaining to the
usage and application of information and advice presented in this book
without permission from your physician.

CONTENTS

CONTENTS

INTRODUCTION

A story from the doctor's office

You are sitting in front of me, shy and confused.
You gaze at the floor, the corners, and it seems as if you are
fleeing and disappearing under my feet.
Your tight dark clothes silently emphasize your slimness.
You are neither girl nor woman.
Your heart skips a beat when you look at me for an instant.
Your lifeless blue-gray eyes, neither alive nor dead.
Your face but a white mask.
Your trembling lips still talk. They are the only thing that
moves, quivering, with painful breaks. You look as if you have
no desire to talk, but you know that you must, and to some
degree, you want to.
You seem to me like a song never sung before, with the
potential of being the right one.

We are alone in the office, just the two of us, for the first time.
You are telling me about yourself.
The words are familiar, ones I have heard so many times
before.
Your story comes out in a quivering whisper, with hope in
your eyes.
It sounds naive and childish, but I know how dangerous it is.
I have seen the consequences – long-term, ugly, and painful.
As if I was looking through a transparent piece of paper with
some writing in your young hand.
An accidentally signed, long-term contract of suffering
between you and yourself, signed in a secluded spot one dark

morning when you could not continue the same way any longer.
A contract with no parties to it. One in which you have not considered the possibility of its cancellation or renouncement.
Only a stamped confirmation. For pain.

With your immense desire to become more beautiful, you innocently stepped into bulimia's path.
It being cunning and you young,
It dangerous and you vulnerable,
It experienced and you helpless,
It grabbed you, sucking you into its greedy guts.
You became its new, carefully watched prey.
But when you realized this, it was already too late. You resisted and fought, while sinking ever deeper.
Believing that luck was at the end of your journey, you roamed the wild.
At the end of your wits, you knew – you could not continue alone.
You need help now.
Finally, you admit it and accept everything. You have given up on the lies.
You want a better life to replace the bad one.
You have had enough of the same old tune. You feel that a new song can be recognized only by a happy heart.
That is why you plead for the cancellation of your own contract.
I have to tell you, it isn't easy to cancel. Zealously written when you were ready for it all, it has turned into a hard rock.
Success can be reached only through cooperation – with me and with everyone who loves you.
Determination, patience, and your new faith will be decisive.

Cancellation is difficult, but not impossible.
It is called LOVE, and consists of ACCEPTANCE.
If you embrace yourself with all your heart – you will fly.
If you merge Life and Goodness into one – you will succeed.
The universe will bow and ask you to dance.
You will dance to the rhythm of the clouds and the stars, and each circle you make will create another day.
The smile from your soul will destroy the darkness, careless mornings will begin to shine, and you will know then that you are healthy again.
I will rejoice as well, for having shown you the way.
For I will have taken a little sad PRINCESS on a secret path to happiness.
On the road, she turned into a WARRIOR.
Once we reach our goal, the gentle hand becomes strong.
Before me, calm and happy, stands the WINNER.

Message and its meaning

Bulimia is an insufficiently recognized pandemic spreading quietly throughout the world. It threatens the health of young women at the threshold of maturity.

Methods of treating and organizing people with eating disorders, particularly those with bulimia and anorexia, have not yet been adequately established. My primary goal is to contribute to the elimination of the atmosphere of secrecy and misunderstanding surrounding bulimia and anorexia that identify them as "modern" and "unnecessary" diseases.

This book is intended primarily for women, as the occurrence of eating disorders is much higher among women than men.

It is dedicated to young women who have lived with bulimia for years and who are running out of energy while fighting its daily torture. I want them to know that they are not alone in their suffering and that help is out there. This book sends them the message that bulimia is no one's fault, and certainly not their fault, because all their wrong decisions were made with the best intentions. These young women acted and lived in the best way they knew how. However, problems arose because their *life experience was wrong and insufficient*, just like that of their parents and their surroundings.

I entirely understand their "hunger" for a happier life, but they need to realize that extremism, perfectionism, and obsession are definitely not the right way to find happiness.

This book is also useful for the parents and friends of the patients, giving them advice as to the type of assistance they can and should provide.

Besides the patients and those closest to them, I also wrote this book for all those who are aware of the secret connection between eating disorders and painful emotions. Negative emotions – fear, depression, shame, and insecurity – are indicators that lead to the main problem these young women have in common: dissatisfaction with their own lives.

Working with bulimic women, I have often had the feeling that they do not live in reality, that they vegetate in a state of unexplainable expectations and hopes. It seems that they ban themselves from living in the present, because they must first complete preparations for some other, exceptional life that is unknown to others, which they believe they will begin living once they are perfectly ready for it. They show no interest in the years they have wasted due to bulimia. Never have I encountered remorse nor sorrow for the time lost in the disease

– as if time was of no importance. They have always behaved as if they will live forever, and as if they had all the time in the world to spend.

They do not show the slightest care or tenderness for themselves. They are full of hatred and contempt for their bodies, and they always seem to create an atmosphere of fear and despair around them.

Their words are always harsh, always ready for pressure and self-punishment. They demand the impossible from themselves, without mercy – a life in absolute perfection. As if otherwise, due to their imperfection, they would be held accountable and undergo a cruel punishment from a court known only to them.

My inspiration to write this book

Research on medical problems pertaining to eating disorders has always been the focus of my professional and personal interest.

Since I have a genetic predisposition for easy and fast weight gain, which I have, unfortunately passed down to my daughter (my son luckily inherited his father's "slim" genes), my motivation to investigate topics related to weight has always been strong and constant.

I have dedicated most of my medical practice and practically all my free time to gaining a better understanding of the complexity of eating disorders and finding new ways to overcome them.

This book is the result of my thirty years of medical experience, during which I have continuously kept track of new medical, philosophical, and psychological theories.

What has motivated me all along has been my aspiration to

discover an efficient and practical solution for a happy and satisfied lifestyle. I have always attempted to find satisfactory answers that would yield excellent practical results, and would not confuse and deceive people, as was previously the case.

This is how I created my own *Overcoming Bulimia Program*, which leads, in practice, to a healthy and happy lifestyle.

I have acquired valuable experience over the last 10 years, during which time I have spent exclusively treating eating disorders in my private practice in Zagreb.

I decided to write this book after receiving numerous e-mails from desperate bulimic young women who had no one to go to for professional help in the small towns where they lived. This is why it seemed natural to sit down at my computer and teach them about the main principles of mental consciousness, emotional maturity, and spirituality in the form of a book.

The publishing of this book is a logical continuation of the medical work that I consider to be my primary purpose and to which I have dedicated my life – to help sick people find a happier and healthier lifestyle.

My "teaching" work is specifically targeted at providing medical help for victims of various eating disorders.

If you are unsure about the type of dietary problem you have, or if you live in a place with no specialist in eating disorders, this book can be a self-help reference until you manage to see a physician.

It will provide you with an opportunity to comprehend the essence of bulimia and embark on the road to recovery.

I do not expect you to follow my advice blindly, but to analyze what you are reading and come to your own conclusions. Perhaps you will read this book several times – initially just for information, and then again slowly and in detail. Try to realize and understand each significant message, then try

experimenting freely with my statements – try them out and test them. In doing so, you will expand your mental boundaries and abandon your limiting convictions, in turn widening your spiritual perceptions about yourself and life in general.
This practice itself will help you find the real truth, and it will therefore become your teacher.

Because it teaches the important principles of a healthy diet and a positive attitude towards life, this book efficiently supports all forms of psychotherapy, with no adverse effects on health. That is why it can also be useful during each medical treatment. In short, this publication does not exclude physicians and treatment – on the contrary, I recommend it, for the book complements their work.

When treating bulimia, this book can also come in handy for physicians. It provides advice and psychological help to patients 24 hours a day, which is a valuable aid in overcoming the potentially dangerous time between weekly medical visits.

I have applied the Overcoming Bulimia Program in my medical practice for years, and it has always yielded positive results – either an improvement in the patient's health, a long period of remission, or a full recovery.
This Program has enabled numerous female patients of mine to regain a normal lifestyle after long-term crisis and illness; to return to school, eventually graduating from their university of choice; or to successfully integrate into a work environment. Success did not depend solely on the length of treatment, but also on the important fact that these patients managed to transform their system of negative attitudes, replacing them with new, positive, and efficient ones.
Those who managed to see themselves and their lives from a

wider perspective with my assistance, realized the truth about life and became open to change. They underwent a *spiritual transformation* of sorts, freeing themselves from the tyranny of their own ego, becoming "reborn" as free and authentic persons.

Goal

The main goal I wish to achieve with this book is to teach you to always feel good about yourself – regardless of the circumstances surrounding you!

This basic positive feeling about yourself is something each one of you had in early childhood, and if you are able to remember it, you will clearly understand what you have lost with this disease.

The precondition for attaining this goal is going back to your authentic identity, returning to your lost "true self". This will renew and strengthen a significant spontaneous feeling of inner peace and satisfaction.

These wonderful feelings had existed in you since birth, and in some past stressful situation you recklessly disrupted and lost them. This essential loss quickly caused other significant losses, such as the ability to rejoice and have faith in your own personal value.

With these losses, you opened the door, unintentionally, for bulimia to enter your lives.

In order to overcome bulimia and turn back into a healthier and happier version of yourselves, you must first understand the essence of your problem and then decide and learn to think in a new way – in an "anti-bulimic" way. Perhaps you will have to reassess and change a number of things in your perception of life, since you will come to the conclusion that they were imposed by your surroundings and are not a result of your experience.

The desired change, expressed by positive feelings and healthy everyday behavior, will be achieved only with the *strengthening of new – different – mental attitudes.*

With the contribution of such positive mental energy, your entire life will be more meaningful and happier.

The Overcoming Bulimia Program is based on the following important realization – that life experience is formed individually, based on the nature of our convictions.

The precondition for recovery is thus a permanent change in the basic perceptions of life from the existing negative (or losing) perceptions, to positive (or winning) perceptions.

To do this, a complete transformation of consciousness and basic perceptions must take place.

This is a significant mental jump ahead, which should, with its energy, eliminate the thick layers of your ego and shed light on your authentic identity.

Everyone wants positive changes, but do not fool yourselves – if you are unable to successfully "decode" the series of events, the process of transformation is difficult and oftentimes unsuccessful.

On the other hand, once you are familiar with the "codes", become aware of them, and accept them, every personal change becomes possible.

You will definitely need help in the transformation process ahead of you, but you must first clearly understand your problem. I will describe the essence of bulimia in detail for this purpose, and hopefully, this will give you the courage to undergo this significant transformation with my help.

Therefore, if you truly desire a positive change, I am offering my services as a guide and interpreter in your transformation to a new life.

You will develop the ability to create an inner feeling of emotional pleasure, and a basic good feeling in a variety of situations in your life, pleasant and unpleasant.

We will travel together. I will lead you carefully, and if you are determined to follow me, bulimia can disappear from your life in just two weeks.

We will walk slowly, taking small steps, but you must not skip any – they are all equally important.

If your parents or partners want to join you, they are welcome, since all support is important, and they will learn things, too.

During this transformation, you will form a new you, the one you desire to be. You will then learn to love yourself unconditionally and take care of yourself always.

Finally, we will make important decisions together, based on your new discoveries. These decisions will form new roads, leading you to your desired future.

Please read this book not only with your eyes and mind, but foremost with your heart – that is where secrets are usually hidden.

PART ONE
BULIMIA IS NOT A DESTINY

What exactly is bulimia?

Bulimia is a characteristic, acquired personality disorder, affecting all levels of personality – spiritual, mental, emotional, and physical.

Spiritual disorder in bulimia – The affected person loses contact with her authentic, true self and consequently with her basic trust in life as a source of happiness and well-being. This contributes to the disease due to wrong beliefs the person has about herself and her life, implying that she is rejected, unloved, and abandoned.

Mental disorder in bulimia - A "new" personality develops in place of the person's repressed authentic personality, subject to a critical ego, forcing its victim into obedience. She is soon convinced that the only reason for her unhappiness is her "weight", and losing weight becomes the only way for her to be happy again. Controlled by her ego, the young woman comes up with cruel strategies for weight loss, tries them all, and finally settles on the bulimic path, which provides the desired result while granting her the freedom to overeat, rather than forcing her to starve.

Emotional disorder in bulimia – Negativistic and contradictory commands by the ego create a range of negative emotions in the patient: fear, despair, self-hatred, depression, sorrow, disappointment, feelings of guilt, and the like. Frequently, the ultimate result is self-injury (cutting the skin with a razor blade, pulling out one's hair), while even suicide attempts are not uncommon.

Physical disorder in bulimia – Negative emotions result in negative activities, demonstrated by typical bulimic behavior – alternating periods of overeating and compensation by "cleansing" the system (vomiting, excessive, and obsessive exercising or laxative use). This results in the physical "suffering" of the system, expressed as disorders of significant metabolic processes:

- imbalance in the concentration of important electrolytes in the blood (e.g. potassium, magnesium, iron, calcium) due to inadequate diet and vomiting, which in turn leads to heart disorders, anemia, and porous bone structures, expressed as osteopenia and osteoporosis;
- irregularity in the supply of vitamins to cells caused by an inadequate diet;
- excessive muscle disintegration caused by insufficient protein intake;
- endocrinologic disorders (pituitary, ovaries, thyroid, pancreas) caused by malnutrition, expressed most often as a long-term absence of menstrual periods and consequently, sterility;
- disorder in the functioning of numerous organs (stomach, intestines, liver, kidneys) caused by insufficient and inadequate diet;
- loss of teeth and loss of tooth enamel caused by gastric acid from vomiting;
- hair loss;
- seriously weakened immunity, with the possibility of developing a number of illnesses.

Long-term experience has taught me that there are two forms of bulimia:

Mental bulimia in *naturally slim* young women, where the problem is primarily "in the head",

and

Metabolic bulimia, in *actually overweight* young women, where the problem lies in metabolic disorders and a genetic predisposition to weight gain.

While the *first group* imagined their weight problem (which did not exist in reality) and believed in it as an excuse for their problems and failures in life, the *second group* developed bulimic strategies for a purely practical reason – to handle their actual weight gain problem.

Accordingly, a physician's approach to each type will be different.

Since a member of the *first group* primarily has a serious mental disorder together with an insignificant metabolic one, the therapy for this group will focus on psychotherapy.

On the other hand, therapy for the *second group* will begin with nutritional therapy, the goal of which is to balance out their metabolism, while psychotherapy will be a complementary component.

These two types represent only initial and introductory approaches to bulimia, as they merge over time and develop common characteristics, both mental and physical.

The overall result of a bulimic disorder is the disappearance of the former, authentic, healthy, and happy person. This person is replaced by a new, unaware, and helpless look-alike who, having lost her authenticity, also loses her sense of security and joy for life. She becomes entirely subject to the tyranny of her ego, deliberately making the wrong decisions in order to maintain control.

Convinced that she can receive love and be happy only through her own determination, she is entirely focused on a useless battle with herself and her natural needs.

False perception of life

Nonprofessionals, especially parents, see the essence of bulimia as "a small misunderstanding" – where young women become bulimic because someone has falsely convinced them that they are overweight. Parents usually think their daughters have been made to believe that being overweight is the true reason for their failure in life, and that weight loss is the right path to happiness.

Moreover, parents think young women will realize their mistake as soon as they are weighed by their physician, and told that they are wrong, their weight being normal.

Unfortunately, this never happens because the issue in bulimia is not one of persuasion and a superficial misconception, but a pathological change in the entire personality.

All eating disorders – excessive weight, obesity, binge eating disorder, bulimia, and anorexia – have a number of common characteristics. These range from depression and negative emotions to consequential obsession and addiction. This is why the basic principles of therapy for all of these disorders have similarities as well.

How a person will look and behave primarily depends on her inherited genetics; however, the significance of the psychosocial framework in which she grew up should never be downplayed.

The basic attitudes a person has and believes in will always, without exception, indicate how that person sees herself and how she imagines her place in life, and point to her unconscious convictions about life in general.

Only self-evaluation matters in regard to any accomplishment, which is why thoughts, feelings, and behavior are adjusted accordingly.

Different opinions are heard, but they are immediately subject to an entirely subjective evaluation by a subconscious court – facts and reality do not influence the decision.

It is only the evaluations, beliefs, and convictions of the "inner child", or our subconscious court, that make decisions about life.

All victims of obesity, bulimia, and anorexia have a common issue – a wrong and typically distorted basic perception of life. Summarized, the following symptoms are the most important:
• uncertainty about one's own personal value,
• lack of confidence in one's own abilities,
• fear of the future (life).

While normal people for the most part live spontaneously and carelessly, resolving their problems in stride without much fuss, obese persons, or those convinced they are obese, turn even the smallest problem into a "global issue", and their experience is much more stressful and serious than it should be.

At the same time, these people are exceptionally, even pathologically ambitious, but hide this by belittling and criticizing themselves. Their ambition is still clearly visible in their tendency to attain extreme perfectionism and their aspirations to control both their lives and their surroundings.

A basic distrust of life, acquired in childhood and usually

passed down by their parents, will subjectively turn everything they experience in life into a red light of danger, forcing them to try and attain full control by panic, although at the same time they have no faith in their own abilities and values.

All of my obese, bulimic, and anorexic patients, without exception, showed constant and very expressed extreme negative emotions (fear, depression, distrust, and insecurity), which led me to persistently focus my research on this.

I believe many of you are familiar with the same or similar emotions, and that deep inside, you recognize and understand them. I am sure you are beginning to understand the immense importance of these feelings in the onset and development of the disease.

Since only big, magnificent wishes and visions (never small and ordinary ones) cause anxiety and a fear of failure in an intelligent person, I truly believe that bulimia (like other eating disorders) settled in precisely due to a pathological desire among young women for a perfect life – without problems or failures, filled exclusively with love, happiness, and achievements.

At the same time, their lack of belief in their own abilities and the constant fear of reality throw them into a twister of depression, widely opening the door to bulimia and other disorders.

Extreme acts by bulimics (overeating, vomiting, excessive exercise, and cleansing with laxatives) are simply symbolic acts, in their desperate attempts to find the perfect life they desire, whatever the cost.

A comprehensive solution to this painful conflict between a desire to have a perfectly happy life on one hand, and a huge existential fear on the other, is possible only by modifying the wrong attitudes, and such a change is possible only through a positive mental and spiritual transformation, which I will describe in detail later on.

Bulimia as a "female issue"

I believe the reason for an incomparably more frequent eating disorder among women than men stems from the unequal and degrading relations between women and men.

The majority of (traditional) men show no interest in the rights and needs of the female population, because their existing superior position suits them perfectly well.

Are you aware of how men think today?

They see life as an interesting game with predetermined rules – a game to be played well in order to defeat the opponent. They do not count on others. In their opinion, everyone must take care of themselves.

They resolve their problems in stride and charge a lot for success. They respect an honorable fight, without the need to humiliate the opponent – defeating them is enough. If the opponent is down, it is enough to let them rise, but they do not offer a helping hand.

What is important is to be among the powerful to prove their value.

Prove to whom?

Primarily to other men, and consequently to us, women.

They will join forces to eliminate capable and demanding women from every competition, especially if the reward is power or money.

Strong women intimidate them – they prefer lovely and submissive ones, always in the shadows and without demands. Men do not reveal their feelings. They believe feelings are overrated and insignificant, even unnecessary. Fast decisions and the protection of the position they have attained, that is important, but no emotions, please!

For such men, the female abundance of emotion is a huge nuisance, for they perceive women as complicated and unreasonable.

They typically declare an intelligent woman to be childish and immature, ignoring female emotions. They show attention to women only when necessary or when it matters to them – usually for entertainment and sex. And even then, they remain distant, on their male side.

Few men find their way into a female soul and respect what they discover there. Even fewer among them open up their own soul in turn and return a smile. And the rarest of them all are those who offer their hand and wipe away a female tear.

Today, women no longer accept living in this kind of world.

They refuse to be the half of mankind that is sentenced to life in the shadows and whispers.

Few women dare to speak up clearly, let alone demand or claim something.

Men do not hear these voices, or pretend not to, conveniently avoiding answering, explaining, or giving something back.

They have raised the price of power so high that it is inaccessible to women.

It is always easier to silence female voices than to understand them.

The easy way out for men is to refuse to understand rather than to build a partnership, and to hide behind their power.

This is particularly hard for sensitive female feelings to cope with. Women refuse to accept male cruelty and indifference. They want a relation that is gentle, close, and primarily based on mutual respect.

All the men in a woman's life – her father, brother, boyfriend, husband, and son –play a significant, even decisive role in her life.

The most important person in a little girl's life is her father, as he is the first man she loves with all of her heart. A father's love or indifference is an important determinant, providing an explanation for all her subsequent relations with men. This is why the deepest sorrows of daughters stem from cold or aggressive fathers.

In the modern world new, different men are needed – true partners to women, who are no longer their masters. They have to show their emotions and use them to develop relationships based on reciprocity and respect.

Unfortunately, women are still not getting partnerships and true understanding from men, forced to endure the cruel male world and survive in it as best they can. Many are unaware of how to do this, since when it was time to teach them, they had no one to learn from. Watching their mother suffer because of demanding husbands and selfish colleagues at work, they too learned, in their early childhood, to hide their pain and began to suffer.

The more sensitive a young woman's nervous system is, the stronger her emotions, and the more developed her intellect, the higher her often unrealistic expectations from life will be, frequently unrealistic, in turn leading to a higher probability of developing a disorder or addiction.

This makes hypersensitive girls more susceptible to severe and deep suffering that could entirely change their life.

Lacking knowledge, wisdom, and life experience at such an early age, in their emotional crises they easily show naiveté and submissiveness. And in such a state of overemphasized infantile despair, they are too ready to make hasty decisions and to enter into risky and dangerous situations.

Whenever they are misunderstood by their father, they suffer immensely.

Since girls are gentle beings with unlimited trust in their parents, their hearts full of love want to forgive their father immediately, and simply assign all the blame to themselves. Suffering without a reason, they readily assume responsibility for this self-inflicted suffering. They wait constantly, persistently hoping to find evidence of the parental love they desire, unsure all along whether they deserve it.

Belief in the existence of parental love determines the value and quality of all other relationships later in their life.

Just a shred of doubt, even once, is enough for them to immediately lose faith in themselves, to completely discard everything – their goodness, beauty, and intellect – all of their valuable qualities. Submerged in this pain early in life, they abandon logic, ready to punish and shun themselves.

Frequently they hate themselves to a point where they subconsciously condemn themselves to disease.

This is how bulimia most often begins.

The *motive* for the onset of bulimia can always be found in the girl's closest *surroundings* during her childhood.

The *cause* for the onset of bulimia can always be found in her *relationships* with people who are important to her. And at this young age, her most important relationships are her *family relationships*.

In assessing the probability of developing bulimia, the crucial issue is therefore how much unconditional love the girl received in her family (if any), and whether she has developed a sense of self-confidence.

This always depends exclusively on her parents.

Her wider surroundings and their influence will become important to the girl only later, again depending on the amount of love, security, and support she has first obtained from her family.

Gender significance in bulimia

Have you ever wondered why only girls suffer from bulimia? Are teenage boys not going through the same temptations and crises in adolescence?

I believe the answer lies in the genetic and social differences.

Girls, due to their natural role as future mothers, are genetically more fragile and self-sacrificing, and therefore, emotionally more vulnerable. Boys, on the other hand, are genetically hunters and defenders; accordingly, this makes them less stable emotionally and more physically active.

Girls are much more susceptible to parental authority, and today also to standards set by the media, since the opinion and affection of their surroundings is exceptionally important to them.

Moreover, numerous parents, primarily fathers, raise their daughters with the aim of making them kind, obedient, and agreeable. Having the desire to please, girls learn the habit of experiencing their emotions passively, suppressing them as undesirable.

Boys, on the other hand, are raised with the aim of becoming strong and stable men, with confidence in themselves, and without giving much thought to the opinions of others. Because of such a parental attitude, boys will reach efficient decisions in a crisis, act fast, and successfully resolve stress. As they are much less susceptible to the pressure of emotions and are genetically much less sensitive, boys will minimize their feelings, will deal with them with ease, and will not suppress them. Boys react only to direct and strong criticism, while not noticing subtle objections, expressed with looks and minor gestures, as opposed to girls. Their reactions to verbal attacks are impulsive and defensive, without pain or withdrawal as those of girls.

Even when they are exposed to suffering in their childhood, they will sooner turn to alcohol or drugs for consolation than to desserts, as girls do, since the soothing effect of food is too mild for their robust temperament.

The few boys that do suffer from bulimia or anorexia are visibly gentler and more insecure than their peers, revealing their emotional personality, which is typically similar to a feminine personality, even before the onset of the disease. The same instructions I give girls in this book will work for boys as well.

The psychological profile of a bulimic person

Another important question: "Why do only some girls suffer from bulimia, while others do not?"

Depending on their age, how they were raised by parents, and their current social circumstances, all girls and young women with a predisposition for disorder will, due to ignorance, deliberately or not, eventually become bulimic. None of them consciously decided to become sick; they were only looking for a quick fix for their problems. We can understand that such wishes and intentions are normal and human.

With the best intention of overcoming a crisis and easing their pain, they behaved and acted as best they knew how in the given situation.

Since every girl has a unique emotional system and pattern

of thinking, each one accordingly carries within her all of her special expectations about the future and her entire life.

These expectations were gradually formed in childhood and are very specific and different for each girl. They depend on a whole range of different factors: genetic predisposition, how they were raised, parental expectations, intellectual potential, the influence of their surroundings, social and material conditions, local customs, standards set by the media, etc.

Based on all these numerous influences, each girl will form her own specific priorities, principles, and standards in life.

Just as certain individuals will engage in specific sports because they have the appropriate physical and mental constitution for that sport, only persons with a specific set of psychological features will have a predisposition for the onset of bulimia.

This is precisely why we can talk about common psychological characteristics representing the *psychological profile of a bulimic person*. These characteristics are for the most part genetically conditioned– through the existence of a specific, genetically determined imbalance of certain chemical substances in the brain (I will discuss this in detail later). This explains why one daughter in a family will have bulimia, while the other, in similar social circumstances, remains psychologically stable and healthy.

These specific psychological characteristics are gradually expressed from early childhood, but their intensity is fully visible only in adolescence and puberty.

Bulimic young women have the following *common* characteristics:
- they are extremely unstable emotionally;
- they are introverted, keeping all their emotions "bottled up";
- they are dissatisfied with everything about themselves;
- they are overly negative in their reactions to and criticism of

the acts of others;

- they conceal their impulsive emotions, being unable to express or reveal them, hiding and suppressing them deep inside;
- they suffer from inferiority complexes, which makes them constantly tense, frustrated, and psychologically stressed;
- more than anything else, they desire affection and the approval of their surroundings;
- they are excessively interested in the opinions of others;
- they are vain, as they cannot stand criticism and are offended easily;
- they are moody, their moods swing according to the circumstances surrounding them;
- they are clearly intelligent, curious, and well-read, and they love to learn;
- they usually rank among the best students in school;
- they are very ambitious;
- more than anything, they desire to be the best and the first in everything they do, although this is concealed from the outside world;
- they always expect the maximum from themselves and are disappointed easily;
- they tend towards extreme perfectionism and are never satisfied with their achievements;
- they have a hard time handling failures, needing a long time to recover from them;
- in case of failure, they often turn to self-hate and different types of self-punishment;
- they live according to the *all or nothing* principle, due to their tendency to have extreme thoughts and uncompromising attitudes;
- they tend to change moods frequently, with depression being their most common psychological condition, dominating

their clinical picture;
- their state of depression usually becomes their *customary and permanent state of mind.*

Bulimic depression can be:
- *"passive"* (lethargy, inactivity, apathy), or
- *"active"* (restlessness, anxiety, panicky aimless activity, obsessive acts, etc.).

Consequences of "passive" depression include not leaving the house, oversleeping, withdrawing from contact with others, constant TV watching, giving up on responsibilities, personal hygiene, clothes, and looks;

Consequences of "active" depression include obsessive exercise, aggression, the tendency to pick fights, insomnia, and self-injury (cutting one's skin with a razor blade, pulling out one's hair, scratching, pinching, and the like).

Depression in bulimia frequently leads to suicide attempts (mostly unsuccessful, being more calls for help; unfortunately, however, they are sometimes successful).

It is important to stress that bulimic young women are genuinely:
- humane, ethical, and truthful;
- intolerant of injustice, lies, and hypocrisy;
- ready to forgive, but very strict and extremely critical of themselves;
- unable to cope with their own and others' suffering and humiliation;
- exceptionally empathic and ready to help others, although they usually lack the energy for it.

It is easy to conclude from the list above that bulimic young women are exceptional personalities – intelligent, imaginative, and generous.

It is therefore tragic that they are their own worst enemy, as their overemphasized perfectionism needlessly makes their lives difficult.

They expect a lot from others, but their highest and most unrealistic expectations are from themselves.

Life is not easy for anyone with this combination of psychological characteristics, because their perception of life is inflexible and too serious.

It has always been difficult and painful for me to watch intelligent, good, and beautiful young women with bulimia suffer and torment themselves needlessly.

PART TWO
MARTA'S STORY

We will continue our narrative with a story about Marta. That will give you the best insight into the life of a typical bulimic girl.

Marta is the main character of the story – a fictional person, a combination of a number of girls I have treated for bulimia over the last 10 years.

I believe this story will be useful for you, that it will give you insight into bulimia, and that you will recognize yourselves in the story.

And now, quiet please, the story is about to begin!

Marta is twenty years old and lives in one of the student dorms by the Sava River in Zagreb.

Her parents and sister live in Split.

Today she has found out she did not pass her freshman year at law school, but she has not shared this information with anyone yet.

Marta rooms with Ana, a successful and ambitious dentistry student from Labin.

Everything Marta is unsuccessful at, Ana accomplishes with ease. She is slim and beautiful, and has passed all the exams in her freshman year. She is a happy and content person. Naturally, she has a boyfriend, Mario, a handsome and intelligent student of computer science.

Marta has a boyfriend as well, but he is in Split, so she feels lonely. Moreover, when she compares him to Ana's Mario, her poor Tom does not stand a chance. He barely made it through high school and has no intention of studying anything else in this lifetime. He works as a waiter in a modern coffee shop, has a large circle of friends, and wants nothing more from life. They have been a couple for three years now, and Marta has a feeling they are more friends than a couple in love. There has been no chemistry between them for a while, but they are still together for company and out of habit.

Marta is beautiful too, but has never been aware of it due to her insecurity. On the contrary, she has always been convinced that all other girls were prettier than her. The numerous freckles on her face have always made her life miserable. Interested looks by passers-by usually make her blush, since she is clueless of the fact that it is precisely her cute freckles, blue eyes, and fiery red hair that make her special to look at.

Whenever her mother stroked her copper-red curls, she thought her mother was feigning affection. It was as if she was comforting her for being so different from Helena, her sister, two years her senior. Helena has always been happy about herself and her surroundings. She never had any big plans for herself and lived a comfortable life with her parents, working as a secretary and spending her free time with friends on the Riva, Split's seaside promenade.

Marta, on the other hand, was always different.

She was different and distant from others – as if she did not belong to anyone or any place.

Gentle and hypersensitive, she has always doubted her own qualities. Unsure of herself, she frequently wonders whether she is worth anything at all and whether she deserves to be loved at all - by her parents, her friends, or a lover. Life seems too complicated, as if it is all happening just to her.

As a child she had already decided to do her best in order to meet the expectations of her strict parents.

She wanted to remain Daddy's favorite forever and see the sparkle in his eyes when he looked at her.

She mostly lives in her own head, constantly in thought, and not noticing that she is slowly distancing herself from reality.

She inherited this perception of life from her father, as he only cared about intellectual things. He ignored emotions and physical contact, considering them to be overrated, dangerous, and useless.

Marta does not remember him ever telling her anything about looks, the enjoyment of life, satisfaction, or joy. He never showed any emotions or even talked about them, as if they were something embarrassing and unnecessary. It seemed as if he had had emotions at one time in the past, but had decided, for reasons unknown to others, to suppress and reject them, and live without them.

Joy, satisfaction, and pleasure were useless nonsense according to him, typical of lazy and superficial people. Sometimes he would even hint at falling in love and talk about love as a triviality and an obsession of stupid and limited women, which Marta and Helena should never become.

He lived an austere life, behaved accordingly, and raised his daughters the same way.

This did not work too well with Helena, since she did not love him as deeply and obsessively as Marta, and was less vulnerable to his words.

On the contrary, for Marta her father's love and pride were the most important things in the world.

Under her father's influence she became dependent on her own intellect, and thinking was her favorite activity. Constantly overworking her brain made Marta gradually ignore her feelings, of which she was no longer aware. But her feelings did not disappear – they just moved to her subconscious level. From there, like illegal soldiers, they kept sending messages to her body, as her mind was inaccessible. The body would assume these youthful and for the most part, contradictory feelings, creating results that would continually sabotage her mind and its wishes. This explains why Marta consciously wanted one thing and would end up with the opposite. Always looking only for intelligent solutions, Marta was unable to explain to herself why she had no control over her body and behavior. She would frantically think for days on end, but after all that thinking and planning she still lived with the same dissatisfaction and problems.

While she had to earn her father's love, it was different with her mother. Her mother's love was a given, as if the two of them were one, and she did not have to prove herself.

At other times, it seemed as if Mom and Dad loved Helena more than her, without having high expectations of her. In their frequent discussions about the future, their parents would always take the opportunity to indicate that more is expected from Marta. They were indirectly telling her she was smarter and more capable, but to her it seemed like a life-long responsibility.

She feels the pressure from the constant efforts she has invested and the sacrifices she has made, but she likes the idea of promised success and dominance in her small universe.

She certainly does not lack ambition.

Burdened with her own and her parents' high expectations, Marta develops a habit of analyzing everything in detail and going through it on her own. To hide from everyone how much she wants to succeed and hated failures, she begins feigning indifference and hiding every painful feeling.

She is not clearly aware why she does this. The best approach seems to be to analyze all situations on her own, assess them and reach decisions, then to present them to others as sudden and spontaneous.

This was the door she was hiding behind.

She could not stand any criticism, not even a hint of a negative opinion. Insecure as she was, however, she did not believe in positive opinions, either. She never thought that she herself was bad, but that others were better and more successful than her.

She could not comprehend how others resolved their problems in life. She expected a "manual for a happy life" to appear from somewhere, with precise instructions for every situation, and a detailed description of how to live without weaknesses and mistakes. She wanted to be perfect in everything, so that everyone would notice how unique and valuable she was.

These life-saving instructions never came, and she painstakingly made up ways of surviving in a world she saw as overly demanding and ruthless.

She did not believe in herself, but she did believe in others. And others were very capable of taking care of themselves, frequently at her expense. In her perfectionism she was the ideal victim, being so easy to hurt.

She remembered preschool, where her toys would always be taken away. Other children would be rude and grab them from her, and being gentle and timid, she would not fight them.

Children nicknamed her Chubby, for her round and always red cheeks. The nickname embarrassed her, but as always, she would not react. She did not speak up even when her family began calling her that – as if she silently agreed. Daddy would frequently repeat that being so round, she looked exactly like his sister. But her aunt had always seemed so monstrously fat and ugly.

Marta showed nothing, revealed nothing, and pretended to be strong. This became her main strategy. The rule was to ignore the rage and anger inside her. The thing to do was to suppress them deep down and smile.

She believed no one had to know how she felt inside.

Growing up in such a rigid and limited world, Marta had become a perfect actress over time. Her own insecurity made her bitter, she gradually became secretly convinced she was worth less than others, and she began to suffer.

No one, least of all her parents, was aware that a completely different person was hiding behind the cute figure of a smart girl, one that was scared, insecure, and had an inferiority complex.

Even with all this, the of Martha's childhood years passed fairly peacefully.

All along, Martha was never fully aware of the strong positive impression she had on everyone around her.

Just as she underestimated her own values and success in school, she was equally unaware of her physical appearance.

Until her teenage years, her looks did not matter to her much. She felt she looked fine, nothing special. She was clueless as to how charming and beautiful her slender body was, as was her gentle face with its kind and intelligent gaze.

She usually admired her friends and her sister, longing for their straight, smooth hair and thin faces without round cheeks.

She had trouble taming her wild curls with numerous hairpins and rubber bands. That is why she decided it was best to not trust any compliments about her looks.

And things remained the same until she turned thirteen.

Then, a friend from school talked her into attending synchronized swimming practice.

She began swimming in order to be with friends and have fun, but it soon turned out she was talented and could compete. She immediately liked the idea. As a hard-working student, she dedicated all her energy to this challenge, always hungry to succeed and to prove her abilities.

Swimming had soon become Marta's great love, the only thing she believed she could do better than others.

This was a careless and happy period of Marta's life...

And the change that came along was sudden and huge.

Over the summer, after she had already turned fourteen, a boy entered Marta's life, someone who would leave a deep and permanent trace.

One hot noon in July, Marta was going home alone from the beach, in a hurry to meet a relative from Zagreb at the train station. Deep in her thoughts, walking through a pine forest, she did not notice a young man on a bicycle catching up with her and slowing down when he reached her. "I have to tell you something, I am the one hundredth guy in Split to be in love with you."

She looked at him in surprise and shrugged her shoulders in confusion. It was the first time she was ever approached by a total stranger. Not knowing what to do, she continued walking. He followed her on his bike, saying:

"I would like to meet you. My name is Dino. I am 17 and want to study journalism in Zagreb. I spend my summers in Split at my grandma's, and live in Zadar with my parents and sister. I noticed you last summer and asked around about you. Strange, but every guy who knew you was secretly in love with you already. So I joined the crowd. I know your name is Marta and that you are the best student in your school."

Marta picked up the pace, as if she wanted to run, but there was no fear in her. The young man's blue eyes and charming smile made her feel good, but his words seemed completely unbelievable.

"I have to go", she said nervously, "leave me alone".

"OK, I'll see you tonight on the Riva, I'll bring you the prettiest rose from grandma's garden."

He waved good-bye and left hastily, with his long hair flying in the wind.

Marta spent her day as usual, completely forgetting the earlier encounter. In the evening, strolling on the Riva with her guest, she saw Dino standing on the side and waving at her with a red rose.

He smiled at her and her chest swelled with excitement. On their way home, an unknown young man approached them, handing her a red rose and something resembling a letter in a white envelope.

"Dino says hello and has asked that you to read the newspaper he made for you." Before she realized what was happening, the rose and the letter were in her hand and the young man had disappeared.

"Oh, how romantic", said the jealous relative, "I didn't know there were guys out there who knew how to write a love newspaper!"

"I don't know, it must be something dumb", answered Marta, confused, although she felt like she had conquered the world.

Later, in her room, she trembled opening the envelope. Inside was a small newspaper made by hand, densely written in neat, small handwriting and covered with flower stickers. All the titles and texts were dedicated to her, sweet and full of admiration and love. A surge of completely new emotions overtook her young, still immature heart. Dino's romantic figure was before her eyes for a long while that night.

The next evening the same thing happened again - a messenger showed up with two red roses now, while Dino was standing on the side looking at her affectionately. They did not talk again. He never approached her, but the "newspaper" was more wonderful by the day, with stories of interesting travels. And another rose came with it every day.

In one of the "newspapers" he admitted to not having known she was only 14, which had made him uneasy. Being three years older, he had no intention of scaring or bothering her, asking only for permission to write to her. This was the only thing he would allow himself to do.

On the twentieth day, Marta received twenty beautiful red roses and the twentieth copy of the "newspaper". This time she sent something in return with the messenger. It was a white rose bud from her garden for Dino.

Then she hurried home, impatient to read his letter. When she arrived home around 10 PM, the house was dark, as if no one was there. Suddenly the light went on in the living room, and Marta saw her father's face distorted with fury. He had all Dino's "newspapers" in his hand, and tossed them at her face. She made a step back, scared and completely confused, as he was in her face, hollering:

"Where are these letters coming from? Are you having an affair with older men, you - who are only 14? Is this how you are paying us back? How could you do this to us?" Her mother's white and scared face petrified her, but even more so, her silence. Her mother did not even attempt to defend her. Her father's voice was bellowing incessantly: "We entirely trusted you, had the highest hopes and expectations from you, and look at you now – you've turned disgustingly trashy, messing with men!"

"But, Dad," Marta attempted to speak, "I haven't done anything! Please, believe me. I don't even know that boy. He is just sending me this newspaper, that's all. We've never even gone for a walk, he's never touched me, you have to believe me!"

He did not believe her and could not calm down. His hollering and anger turned into a nightmare for Marta that sleepless night. He would storm out of her room, and as soon as she thought he was finally asleep, he would come back, turn the light on again and continue shouting, threatening, and accusing her.

She finally fell asleep at dawn, paralyzed by his threats and heartbroken from his false accusations.

In the morning, as soon as she opened her eyes, Marta instantly remembered the horror of the previous night, and her heart froze with pain and fear. The sunny, golden day suddenly seemed gray and horrible, and her life – so ordinary and peaceful only yesterday – had become a heavy burden that her father had placed on her chest the night before.

Even breathing was painful.

She could not talk for the lump in her throat.

Everything was different, and she felt things would never go back to how they were. Suddenly, she felt 10 years older.

In her mind, she was frantically repeating: "Dad can't stop loving me! I have to prove to him that I am a good girl. I'll be the best, I'll be perfect. I can't live with his contempt. Nothing else matters – I will renounce love and all of my feelings for Dino, I never want to see Dino again. I will renounce everything, everything Daddy dislikes. I will be his little princess, his smart little girl. I will live up to his desires, only to keep his love for me."

Her nights became sleepless, and she spent her days doing homework and swimming. She avoided strolls on the Riva, and all attempts by Dino to send her newspapers and flowers were rejected silently and decisively. Only his pale face and his sad, no longer glowing eyes, were engraved in her memory.

In doing so, that night Marta had unconsciously, without any fault of her own, banned love for herself for a very, very long time.

Without hesitation or a need to choose, she picked her father, keeping him on a pedestal in her life – as the first and most important person she had.

As her first encounter with teenage love was brutally terminated, she had no enthusiasm left for the rest of the summer. She did not go to the beach and avoided the Riva. For the most part, she lived in her room, spending hours reading and thinking.
She became quiet, serious, and lonely.
She never saw or heard from Dino again, except for several desperate letters he sent her through her friends from school, failing to understand why she had pushed him away.

Although she had done nothing wrong, Marta constantly felt guilty. She blamed herself for an imaginary mistake, and started believing in it. Her father's cruel words had cut into her heart and took away all her joy.
In a single day she stopped being a happy girl, and turned into a depressed and unhappy young woman.
Surprisingly for her, she noticed that, unlike her, her father did not attach any importance to the horrible incident and never brought it up again. He behaved as if nothing had happened. In fact, certain that he had accomplished what he wanted – preventing her from falling in love for the first time and from turning her attention away from studying and success in school – he was satisfied and happy. He believed he had done the right thing as a father, but due to his male insensitivity, he was fully unaware of the long-term emotional damage he had caused his beloved daughter.

Over the next few months, Marta mostly spent her days studying, and swimming was the only fun she would allow herself.

She worked hard at practice, sure that she and her partner Sandra could accomplish a lot.

She spent a huge amount of energy, and would eat a lot at home to remain strong.

Her parents, especially her father, warned her more and more frequently to not overeat, but Marta ate carelessly, convinced she would burn all her calories in practice. Moreover, it was pleasant and calming to have a good meal after three hours of physical exercise. Her body was firm, muscular and strong, yet still gracious and slim. She felt good inside her body and did not think about the way others saw her. Winning was what mattered, and it became more frequent over time - first locally, then gradually at bigger competitions, until it was time to compete in a large European tournament.

Marta was 16 at the time.

One Monday during regular check-ups in the club, her coach noticed she had gained weight and began reproaching her about it. Marta did not pay much attention to that, as she felt great, and the increase from 50 to 56 kg did not seem important in view of her height – 170 cm. Unconcerned, she continued eating, until a month before the European competition, when the scale showed 60 kg. The upper limit for her category was 54 kg. The coach was livid. He was shouting for almost half an hour, threatening to replace her with Iva, who weighed only 50 kg and was, according to his words, beautiful and slim, unlike her, who had turned into a real "fat pig".

"If you don't lose 8 kg immediately, forget about the European tournament and you could easily say good-bye to synchronized swimming as well. You do not conform to the weight requirements any longer!" he yelled angrily. "What is your problem, why have you done this to yourself? Can't you stop pigging out?" he went on.

Marta's face was beet red with embarrassment, and her stomach was in knots. She wanted to disappear and die instantly as she was standing there, in her wet bathing suit, which was now squeezing her as if it were steel. She could barely breathe from shock.

It seemed to her that the coach's and her father's face had merged into one – a threatening face despising her and loving her no longer.

The coach went on, and she saw her father's scoffing mouth, saying: "Who would want to look at you this fat! I don't need that embarrassment."

She could not handle the double rejection. She pleaded: "But please, it's not that much! I will take care of it, I promise. I will lose the 8 kilos instantly, I know that. I will stop eating altogether, trust me. Please don't kick me off the team!"

It seemed as if she was begging her father for a shred of understanding and love, begging for something she was naturally entitled to.

She was convinced she had become a fat freak who was disgusting to look at.

She sobbed, trying to get the coach to change his mind, but he was relentless. It was as if he had completely forgotten how important she had been to the club all along.

Not used to accusations, she was paralyzed with horror.

Marta did not know that half an hour earlier the club president had threatened to fire the coach, who had again been drinking before coming to work. She was unaware that she was a good excuse for the coach to vent his frustration on someone else. Experienced from fighting with his wife, he knew exactly what to say to hurt a female soul the most.

Not knowing any of this, Marta blamed herself for everything. She was racked with guilt for having eaten so carelessly for months on end. In her mind, she would tear all that food out of her body, along with her weight, to be empty, clean and slim like before. All her father's warnings to not overeat sounded like accusations in her head.

With her head down, not allowing Sandra to console her, she ran to the locker room, put on her clothes over her wet body, sat on the floor, and cried. There was one thought tormenting her: "I've disappointed everyone. I've disappointed my Dad. I'm a terrible person - I don't deserve any better. I just want to get away from everyone, even from myself . . ."

That day, Marta's world fell apart.

Deep inside, she felt this was the confirmation of her long-time premonition that life was dangerous and scary.

"This is it", she thought, "this is the end of my hopes that working hard, giving my best, and utilizing my talent could ever result in anything good and worthwhile. Whatever I love the most disappears from my life in such a terrible, humiliating way. This is the final proof that I am not worthy of happiness, proof that I am a freak who people can't even look at." She was inconsolable, and when Iva walked in and tried to hug her, infuriated, Marta pushed her away.

With her last strength she screamed in despair: "You'll see, I can lose weight if I decide to! You'll see, and he'll see what I can do. He'll realize they won't get a medal without me. I haven't spent four years in vain for this. There will be no replacement."

She returned home late at night. No one was there. Her sister was out with friends, and her parents were probably visiting neighbors. She was hoping to be able to talk to her mother, who was the only one who could understand and comfort her. With tears in her eyes, she remembered her father's joke that her cheeks were so round her face would burst like a balloon. This was back when he was still proud of her hard work in practice, when it all seemed like benevolent teasing. How confident she had been of herself and her father, and what a mistake that was!

She quickly went to her room, locked the door, and took all her clothes off in front of a large mirror, well-lit by the ceiling light.

She stood calmly waiting for the verdict. Everything she saw seemed huge and ugly.

She did not see the strong and slender figure of her flat belly and beautiful legs, what she saw were sections of grotesquely big thighs, oversized breasts and cellulite everywhere.

Her face looked like a full moon, and she stared at her reflection, scared by what she saw. Turning around, she saw her buttocks, not as they truly were - round and firm, but huge and flabby. She threw herself on the bed, sobbing, disgusted with herself. Her heart was overwhelmed with pain and she felt a rock was on her chest.

Hearing sounds, she knew her parents had returned.

When her mother called her, she came out of the room quietly, her face emotionless, and sat down to eat. She ate like a robot. It was yet another dinner that her mother had been carefully preparing for her for four years. There was always protein at the table – meat, fish, or eggs – a vegetable side dish, big salads, sometimes even whole-grain pasta. Finally, something sweet was served – her mother's home-made cakes or her favorite chocolate – Milka. That food made her feel healthy and gave her strength. From now on, however, it was to be her mortal enemy. She had to get it out of her life.

But no one should notice anything.

She knew her plan would surely not meet their approval. They would consider it drastic and detrimental to her health. But they would probably think differently had they endured what she had gone through. From now on, she would take care of herself, and assume full control over her life. She would not allow anyone to get in the way of her dreams and her happiness. This time her goal was simple and the only one possible: she would become slim and beautiful, proving to everyone that she was the best and irreplaceable. And she would do it fast – in only seven days.

Marta covered her eyes, red from crying, with her hair, and no one noticed a thing.

Her father was engrossed in a game on TV, and her mother was cleaning the kitchen. This is good, she had no intention of breaking down in front of them. Under no circumstances would she disappoint them.

She sat calmly, and a new feeling surged from deep inside her, bringing about a new key decision.

"I will change my diet", she thought, "I will lose weight instantly, to patch up this broken life."

"But how, how?" - screamed a voice inside her, "what are you to do, how will you do this, how should you behave so that others won't notice?"

Suddenly delirious, she clearly saw her answer. The idea overtook her completely, ordering: "just eat like you always have, then get it out of your system and no one will ever notice!"

Inside she was screaming: "OK, my disgusting, fat body. I'll take care of you. You will get nothing, I will leave nothing for you. You have been stuffing yourself all your life. This is a declaration of war between the two of us, and I will win it!"

This idea seemed to take all the burden off Marta's chest, and she felt whole again. "That's it! That is the solution. Eat in front of her parents, pretend everything is fine, then vomit to get rid of the food!"

"Naturally, I'll have to be an actress, but I have mastered that art by now. They will see what I will turn into. Slim and beautiful – in only a few days. They will be shocked to see me, and that jerk, Goran the coach, will apologize and send me to the tournament. Oh, thank goodness I had this idea; at least my brain never lets me down. I'm so glad to have remembered how Ivana's sister used to throw up when she fell in love, and it was worth it, she lost weight and turned into a real beauty!"

Marta forced herself to finish dinner, but skipped chocolate that night. No one noticed anything. Her parents were preoccupied with their usual evening activities.

She got up from the table, went to the bathroom and locked the door. Turning around, she met her frightened gaze in the mirror.

"Now, my darling, you will throw up everything, wash your face and brush your teeth, and it will be as if you did not have anything to eat. An empty stomach and a hungry body will burn the fat deposits", she said to herself.

"Before I go to bed, I will weigh myself naked", she thought. "I have to bring the scale to my room, I'll tell mom the coach asked me to. Tomorrow morning I will weigh myself again to see how much I've lost. That's how I'll know how to continue."

The first time she induced vomiting was not easy.

She pushed her fingers, almost her entire fist, into her throat. Her stomach contracted, but nothing happened. She would not give up. The food inside her was an enemy she would not tolerate.

She convulsed, groaned, drank lots of water and suddenly the thick, acid mush came up, and into the toilet bowl. She was shocked to see how much food was inside her. The feeling of relief and triumph was overwhelming.

She carefully cleaned everything, washed her face, and brushed her teeth for a long time, as the taste in her mouth was awful, strong and sour.

She composed herself, changed the tortured look that was on her face into a happy one and sneaked back into the living room. At the first available opportunity she said there was homework to do and went to her room.

She was happy with herself. She felt so good, she almost forgot the anger and rage that had tormented her that whole afternoon.

"This is great. Maybe I'll even be thanking Goran one day for his threats – they got me to do something. Nothing else would give me this much strength and the will to do what I have always wanted – an ideal body without a gram of fat."

And that is how bulimia entered Marta's life.

Marta lost 5 kg in less than a week, and then another 4 kg. She was beside herself with joy. Her coach commended her and put her back on the team, but swimming and competitions had lost their charm for Marta. This is why the tournament was not a success, either.

She was obsessed with her looks. Proud of herself, she spent increasingly more time standing on the scale and in front of the mirror. The idealist that she once was turned into a materialist. It became important to be prettier than the other girls, to be better dressed than the others, and to wear makeup. She knew all the latest trends in fashion, followed the stories about the famous stars, and dreamed of fame, wealth, and a life of luxury. Besides having become an expert at reading fashion magazines, she was also an expert at induced vomiting.

This activity became easier and faster.

She gained confidence in her "weight-control" method. Her fear of gaining weight diminished, but she remained cautious, regardless.

It seemed like having discovered a magic formula – eating

whatever and whenever she chose, enjoying her favorite foods as much as she liked, without gaining weight. She would not give her slender figure up for anything in this world.

Envious of her beautiful body, her friends often wondered how she managed to stay slim.

Marta carefully hid her secret, with a story on a healthy and moderate diet always at hand.

Swimming was no longer a sport she liked, only an opportunity to strengthen her muscles and burn as many calories as possible.

Being smart enough to know that some food was necessary to maintain her slim figure, she learned to not empty her stomach fully when vomiting, so that some food would remain inside.

Marta became an expert on food types and calorie counting, deciding after which foods to induce vomiting (fatty and sweet), and which to keep inside (vegetables, fruit, and fat-free proteins).

Her parents were delighted that Marta ate plenty and well, remaining thin. They saw nothing strange in this, although they should have, a long while back.

They never wondered how it was possible that on a daily basis Marta ate much more than her father, who was tall and big, yet remained slim, much slimmer than her sister, who ate much less. They saw the answer in her intense practice, assuming she needed a lot of energy, and never brought it up.

The first six months of Marta's bulimia was idyllic.

She regularly ate meals her mother cooked for her, and regularly vomited more than half of what she ate.

Enough food was still in her for her system to function and to stay healthy, and she felt strong, full, and happy.

She was certain she had full control over all the events in her life, and this made her happy.

In school, she was still among the best students, she felt pretty and successful, while admiring looks from men made her self-confident, perhaps even somewhat cocky.

After six months she felt she could start experimenting.

Since she felt her method worked well against weight gain, she began eating more foods she craved, skipping the cooked meals. Being a good actress, Marta would lie to her mother, saying either that she was tired and would eat later, or that she had eaten at a friend's house.

Over time, her meals became more secretive, her portions bigger and more frequent.

She felt an irresistible need to eat precisely the food that had scared her previously – sweet and fatty: chocolate, cake, ice cream, cream-filled cookies, chips, pastry from a bakery, sandwiches, pizzas, and fast food from McDonald's.

She would start planning those meals in the morning and look forward to them.

She could barely wait to be left alone at home.

Thrilled, Marta would obsess over foods she would eat and the joy it would give her.

She acted like a drug addict, impatient for his next fix.

She would buy her favorite foods in advance and hide them at home.

She took things from the kitchen that her mother would not notice.

Impatiently, she would prepare "feasts" that no one knew about.

The amount of sweets gradually increased over time, making her induced vomiting more thorough.

Enjoying "forbidden" foods became increasingly more

important in Marta's life. Everything else – healthy foods – lost all appeal. She would only eat her mother's cooked meals if there was no way of avoiding them, and would end her day by secretly overeating in her room.

Everything in Marta's life except sweets and overeating had slowly become irrelevant and unimportant.

Acting, hypocrisy, lies, and stealing from her parents had become the only topics in her plans and thoughts.

Because it all happened very gradually and relentlessly, Marta was not aware of the moment in which control over her playing with food was assumed by something much more powerful and cunning than she was.

It seemed like a giant reptile resided in her belly, constantly demanding food and never being full.

She began feeling like a slave, forced to feed her impatient master, with no right to do anything she wanted.

She no longer ate because she wanted to, she was forced to overeat because she no longer had any other choice.

The insatiable craving for fatty, sweet, and starchy foods tormented her incessantly, day and night.

As soon as one eating binge ended, she would quickly induce vomiting, and a new craving would already be showing its ugly face.

The "master" had unlimited power over her.

She often imagined hearing his deep voice giving her orders and scolding her.

The "voice" would tell her she was ugly, fat, unworthy of life. That she needed to try harder, exercise more, lose more weight. No matter what she did, nothing was good enough.

She would swim for two hours incessantly, until she was exhausted, as if threatened by someone. The "voice" would then order her to embark on another eating binge, and another, and yet another.

This would immediately be followed by scolding for stuffing herself with food and horror over the possibility of even minor weight gain.

Fairly soon, her diet consisted exclusively of starving herself and overeating.

Every eating binge would be followed by such guilt, that she instinctively stopped eating until she would be starving, and once she would start eating, she was unable to stop stuffing herself with food, until she would fill up to her throat, and the food would almost came back out on its own.

She had determined her desired weight to be 45 kg, and everything in her life revolved around this number – being either close or far from this goal. Every morning the scale would mercilessly determine her day. Her emotions would swing from one extreme to the other. Euphoric and satisfied when her weight was below her goal, she would get severely depressed on days when the scale showed even a minimal increase over 45 kg.

She despised herself for her weakness for food, and on especially difficult days, her contempt would turn into a strong hatred towards her body. Razor blade scars on the skin of her arms and legs were evidence of this hatred.

It seemed to her that she lived in her own nightmare from which she could not wake up.

Then, there were those exceptionally hard nights when, having overeaten and vomited, life seemed useless to her, and she saw the potential solution to her problems in death.

Communication with people was also characterized by extremes – all or nothing. She was either overly friendly and hyperactive, or was distant and desperate.

Only suffering was her loyal companion. Permanent pain devastated her soul, regardless of what happened around her . . .

Marta spent years in her own private hell. Yet she was still unable to find a solution.

In this state she met Tom. She feigned love she did not feel. Selfishly, she took his love, desperate for feelings she had never experienced.

According to her perfectionist nature, she completed high school as an A student.

Although defeated internally, she still played the well-rehearsed role of a winner for the outside world, so well that no one questioned the image she had created of herself. She had no respect for her qualities and did not recognize them, as there is no room for them in the bulimic lifestyle.

Bulimia ruthlessly seized more control and power over her as days went by, as she struggled to free herself in an ocean of despair, like a tiny fish caught with a big rod.

Much as she tried, she could not satisfy her dark "master". His incessant ridiculing and sneering made her feel ever more helpless.

Feeding her bulimia became Marta's whole-day task, with no break.

It became harder and harder to play the role of a normal girl. She lacked the energy and strength.

Any feeling of satisfaction disappeared without a trace.

All this time, poor Marta had no idea what the problem was. She was not aware that gradually and slowly she was caught in bulimia's net.

She had heard about bulimia, watched it on TV, read about it in newspapers, but never really saw the connection to her problem.

She firmly believed that her "invention" of maintaining weight was authentic, as well as safe and harmless for her health. For a long time she believed she had full control over it. She was certain that she could stop overeating and vomiting whenever she decided to.

Marta had convinced herself that it would be easy to switch back to her earlier diet.

There were days when she wanted that.

There were days when she succeeded in it.

On those days she would carefully select only healthy foods, eat small quantities and invest an effort to keep it inside her.

However, this meant a mutiny against the "powerful master", and he would instantly be livid. He could not stand disobedience. His accusations that she was overweight and ugly would double in force he would make even more fun of her looks, foreseeing her quick surrender and submission.

And usually, he was right. He would regularly win.

Five years later Marta finally realized she had bulimia and admitted it to herself. She had to accept the whole truth.

She was no match for the secret disease that was running her life. She did not know where the disease came from, nor did she understand why. All she felt was its constant presence and the terrible suffering that accompanied it.

The worst of it was that she had no one to confide in, no one to open up to, who would comfort and help her.

To her friends she was still a role model of a healthy and athletic young woman. Telling them the truth about herself was out of the question. She could not stand the thought of their looks of triumph and pity. By ruining her present image she would admit her worthlessness and make their small, ordinary lives look good, those same lives she had belittled in her bulimic arrogance.

She could not confide in her sister, who was obedient and would share the story with her parents immediately.

She wanted to tell her mother everything, but was embarrassed about all those years of lies and deceit. She could not face the pain and disappointment this confession would cause her mother.

Her father was out of the question, especially after the night when she was believed to have deceived him.

The surprising fact that her father was still proud of her was the main reason Marta did not renounce herself and her life.

It was clear to her that she could not resolve the problem on her own, now when she truly wanted to.

She had a genuine desire to save herself from five years of terror in her head, and to cease being an obedient robot, suffering constantly.

"Just like drug addicts need help, I need it as well, I am addicted to food," she thought, afraid that her "master" would discover her intentions and reject them with a sneer.

To go visit her physician seemed to be a good decision. She will understand me, she must have experience with this disorder. Maybe she can prescribe something, and I will stop overeating. I will explain to her what is happening to me, and why I no longer have any control over my behavior. And most importantly, the doctor will keep my secret. That way, I can get better without anyone knowing that I suffered from this embarrassing disease of bulimia." This thought brought her great comfort.

That very same afternoon Marta was in the physician's office, face to face with the doctor she knew since childhood. Red in the face, looking down and with trembling lips, she opened her tormented soul and confessed to her doctor, as she would have done in church. The doctor listened carefully without interrupting until Marta finished her sad story.

Then it was the doctor's turn. Full of hope, Marta waited for consolation and help.

"You were always an exceptionally healthy child", the doctor smiled. "You look perfectly healthy to me still, and I can only envy you your figure. You look perfect – like a cover page model in a fashion magazine", was the familiar sentence Marta had heard so many times before.

"Come over here, I will measure your height and then we will see whether there is reason to panic" said the doctor gently and put her arm on Marta's shoulder.

"You are 170 cm tall and weigh 49.2 kg. Your body fat is 12%. Let me calculate your body mass index (BMI). If the result is between 18.5 and 24, this indicates your body weight is normal. If it is under 18.5, you are thin, but if the result is lower than 17.5, that is anorexic weight."

Marta remembers well the piece of paper with numbers on it, and the calculator in the physician's hands.

"See Marta, this is the formula for calculating BMI.

I will divide your body weight in kilograms with your square height in meters.

Your result is 49.2/2.89, and that is 17.

Hm, this is not good, and the percentage of your body fat is too low, it should be at least 17%.

For your BMI to reach at least 18.5, which is the lowest normal body weight, you should weigh 53.4 kg.

A BMI of 20 represents ideal body weight, and in your case this would be 57.8 kg. This means that your weight should range between 53.4 and 57.8 kg, and that your healthy weight limits are within this range. The percentage of body fat for your age should be between 17% and 23%.

All in all, dear, you only need to gain 4 kg for everything to be perfectly fine again. You will still be slim, don't worry so much, darling. Just eat a healthy diet and don't work so hard during practice. Things will take care of themselves. You will be less tired and nervous, and your psychological hunger will not torment you. Then you will not want to vomit any longer. Just relax, you seem so tense and nervous. A healthy girl, and so worried! I can recommend excellent multivitamins, they will give you extra strength and a better appetite."

The doctor did not seem worried; she seemed to believe the problem would be resolved easily.

Marta was so disappointed she could barely see things around her. She had suffered so much to get to this weight, to not gain an extra gram! Her plan was to go even lower, to 45 kg. And now she was supposed to give up and intentionally gain weight? After everything she had been through? This was absolutely out of the question!

"I did not come here because of my weight! I came because of overeating, vomiting, because of the secret problem that has tormented me for so many years", she thought, furious. She felt she would not get any help, since the doctor did not understand the essence of her problem.

Marta thanked the doctor quickly, and with her head down, left the office.

And so her first attempt to get help failed miserably.

She kept walking the well-known bulimic path, and her days were slow and dull.

Marta hoped going to Zagreb to study would change something, but as it turned out, it was even easier to live with bulimia there. No one watched over her, money arrived regularly, she could eat whatever she liked and go on a binge whenever she felt like it. The only problem was that she would quickly spend her money, mostly on the sugary foods she overate, and would then have to make do with the cheapest junk that could play the bulimic role. She became quite knowledgeable – just a few dollars would buy enough sugary foods in a bakery or a store, and these became the only meals she ate. Her favorite was Chocolino, chocolate cereal flakes that she would make in a huge pot and eat incessantly.

Preoccupied with her bulimia, she completely abandoned her classes and studying.

She would spend days in her room, overeating and vomiting.

She noticed her hair began falling out, her teeth hurt, her tooth enamel was gone, and occasionally she would feel her heart beat too fast, along with pressure in her chest. She was aware that her lifestyle was seriously jeopardizing her health, but she was unable to control her behavior.

She wanted to, but did not know how.

Marta was constantly depressed, nervous, and listless. She was her own worst enemy, for she hated her body, her mind, and her life.

Moreover, none of the colleagues she had got to know were good enough for her. Avoiding people, she rarely went out. On those rare occasions when she did venture out, she would drink a lot, having noticed that alcohol could replace her binge eating. Intoxication had a very similar effect to that of overeating.

When she drank, she would calm down and temporarily forget all of her problems and concerns.

Her feelings of guilt and remorse would surface later, in the process of sobering up with hangovers, which resembled her state after induced vomiting.

More and more frequently she would begin drinking alone at home. Only after she finished a whole bottle of wine would she would fall fast asleep, and in doing so avoid the bitter taste of truth and facing herself.

Marta was in this condition at the time I decided to tell you her story.

Thousands of girls are in this condition throughout Croatia, and millions of others around the world.

Each one lives in her own bulimic chaos, completely misunderstanding her situation, and hoping for a miracle that will save her and show her the way back to a normal life.

PART THREE
BULIMIA REFLECTED IN A MIRROR

Development of the bulimic disorder

Dear readers, now that you have gotten to know Marta, what are your thoughts about her?

Are your stories somewhat similar to hers?

I know, a number of you will say that your problems started differently.

For some, the *trigger* for the onset of bulimia was their parents' divorce.

For others, it was the suffering caused by an indifferent and overly critical father.

For others yet, it was their jealousy of their father's new marriage and new children, which made them feel as if they were no longer loved.

Then there are those who had been criticized by their mother while trying on clothes in a store.

Some young women may have suffered because of their father's drinking and physical abuse or because they had been embarrassed in school when other children made fun of them. It could have been the pain caused by a nasty friend's remark about their waist, a strong feeling of being overweight when boys admire fragile ballerinas, or perhaps the unhappy ending of a great love, interpreted as a result of their excessive weight and worthlessness.

You can continue down the list yourselves.

It is completely irrelevant which painful event was the actual trigger, or the immediate cause that led you down the road to bulimia. All triggers are essentially identical – a *dysfunctional emotional relationship that was extremely important to you*!

Triggers for the onset of bulimia are different and specific for every person, but the cause leading to the onset of bulimia is the same for everyone.

The cause leading to the development of bulimic disorder is always strong emotional stress – a painful psychological "wound", the result of a dysfunctional relationship that is exceptionally important to you.

The consequence of opening this emotional wound triggers such immense psychological pain that the wounded person's authentic (inborn) positive emotional integrity falls apart.

This emotional breakdown provides the ego with a leading role on the mental scene.

The ego immediately initiates changes by creating a new, negativistic identity for the young woman. She becomes incapable of assessing and perceiving of her own life in a realistic fashion; she begins to believe only in her own shortcomings; and she blames herself for everything that happens to her.

Under the tyranny of her critical ego, she accepts extremely negative new beliefs about herself and her life without resistance.

In doing so, unaware and naive, the young woman adopts a defeating false perception of herself and of her place in the world. As of that moment, she starts feeling let down and shunned, which makes her withdraw into depression. She wears various "masks" for the people around her, hiding her hurt feelings and her real condition.

All of these things mentioned above can lead this woman down the road to bulimia only if she has a genetic predisposition for emotional overreacting, resulting in the development of a strong ego.

This is when the ego will "overwrite" the reasonable activities of the mind by introducing automatic, dictated ones, until the victim has fully surrendered. The ego then assumes absolute power over her wishes, having entirely submitted her to its incessant criticism.

Once her ego succeeds in completely overtaking her true identity, fully conquering her positive side, it is easy for the young woman to see herself solely through the prism of insecurity and hatred.

Dominated in this manner, the girl will unconsciously and incorrectly perceive herself as a person unworthy of love, which in turn causes her infinite pain. The bulimic strategy of weight loss will thus become quite attractive to her, resembling a brilliant solution for obtaining what she wants the most – perfect looks – since she believes it is only her looks that can guarantee her a perfect life and perfect relationships with others.

Manipulated to the extreme by her own ego, a bulimic will continue her daily life, unconsciously acting solely upon ruthless and threatening orders from her ego.

The more critical and stronger the ego, the more severe form of bulimia will develop.

The ego will take advantage of every subsequent dysfunctional relationship to cause more pain in its victim and develop an even stronger inferiority complex in her.

Within the process described above, the persistent and cunning ego will not only lead its victim to bulimia, but will also make sure this state of mind is maintained.

My patients have frequently talked about their "negative mind", admitting that it runs their lives, forcing them to go on binges, insulting and accusing them to no end. However, they all failed to understand what this "voice" was, where it was coming from and what its true significance was.

The traits of a bulimic ego

The ego is an artificial, nontransparent cover hiding your authentic mind. It has been tailored and sewn from your birth – with the threads of your first cry, first embarrassment, first deep sigh, first pain, then the second, third, one hundredth, and so – until today.

It also consists of smiles and shreds of happy memories, but their warmth is weak in the lonely nights. Being more intense, pain is always stronger than joy. Tears are warm and burn for a long time, which is why we remember them much longer than laughter.

Every harsh word, every reproach and comparison, every accusing and condescending look, everything that has ever hurt you or even resembled pain – it is all woven into your ego and lives inside you. Your ego has thus become your emotional storage – a dump for your emotional waste. You carry it in your mind, innocently believing that it is your true identity.

During our lifetimes we all develop our own unique ego, with specific positive and negative traits. They depend on our genetic character structure and previous life experiences (particularly during childhood, puberty, and adolescence).

Emotionally stable people will have a less prominently expressed ego and will use more common sense and real facts when resolving their life problems, while emotionally unstable persons will develop a huge and negative ego, pushing back their common sense, and imposing its negative solutions to all their problems in life.

For bulimic patients, who are genetically emotionally extremely weak, the following rule applies: the more susceptible you are to strong emotions (remember that negative emotions are always stronger than positive ones), the more easily your ego will develop into a stronger and more negative one.

This is why, in moments of strong negative emotional stress, your already strong ego obtains a new, even bigger strength and *extreme negativity* (which can even lead you to suicide).

Over the years, this ego becomes your new "true self", and, unaware of its existence, you see the world through its distorted and negative prism. In doing so, you incorrectly assess and interpret your entire reality, and then live according to these negative assessments.

This is the essence of your life with bulimia!

This truth is *the secret of bulimia.*

A bulimic ego is *selfish* – convincing you that you are alone and that no one cares about you. You believe it and think of nothing but yourself. You scheme and devise ways of using nature, people, and circumstances to your advantage. You feel distant from everyone else and abandoned in the fierce fight for survival.

A bulimic ego is *vain* - convincing you that only the best is good enough for you.

A bulimic ego is *perfectionist* – it acknowledges nothing but perfection. Everything less is worthy only of contempt.

A bulimic ego is *compulsive* – it wants everything immediately or gives up entirely.

A bulimic ego is *extreme* – it will never accept compromise. If something is not completely good, it is instantly completely bad.
For instance, to my question of how well she was doing in school, a bulimic patient who was a high school senior replied, "Badly – I'm the second best in my class." It turned out she had straight "A"s and only one B, but that was enough to declare herself a loser.

A bulimic ego constantly *compares* – always at the expense of its victim.

A bulimic ego is always *frightened* - painting the future with the darkest of colors.

A bulimic ego *threatens and blackmails* - the situation is bad, and its worsening is anticipated, so it demands absolute obedience.

A bulimic ego is *critical and resentful* - nothing is ever good enough, and it is constantly looking for something better.

A bulimic ego wants *supremacy* – it is satisfied only when it is on top.

A bulimic ego is *whimsical, fickle, and capricious* - flattering and praising one moment ("You've eaten such a fine meal, you can really enjoy life!"), then scaring and threatening the very next ("It's disgusting how you've allowed yourself to overeat again. You are already as fat as a pig – how much more do you want? You have to go vomit immediately, although it may be too late for you...")

A bulimic ego is *submissive, trendy* and *snobbish* - it easily submits to standards set by the media, it likes to be seen and complimented, it is extravagant and loves shopping.

A bulimic ego is *materialistic and megalomaniacal* – placing great importance on material wealth and supremacy in the form of owning and displaying beautiful and valuable things, as well as enjoying extravagance, entertainment, food, and drink.

A bulimic ego is an *evil master* - it shows no mercy towards its victim; keeping her in its bulimic prison, it tortures the victim to extreme limits - sometimes even to death.

Suppressing emotions in bulimia

Since the lives of girls in puberty and adolescence are still primarily linked to family, it is not surprising that they expect unconditional love precisely from their parents, looking for the first and most important confirmation of their own worth. Due to their vain ego, they will react with hypersensitivity to every sign of disapproval or criticism by parents, even when this is not verbally expressed. An isolated look, condescending smile, or even tone of voice will be enough. Since such a sensitive young body cannot stand the huge emotional pain without serious psychological damage, its mind will automatically switch to "emergency help" in order to get it through this. An occurrence of immense emotional pain will instantly be pushed deep into the subconscious, so as to hide its existence.

In doing so, the person is truly "saved" from the stress endangering their lives, if only temporarily.

Unfortunately, suppressing painful emotions strengthens the ego and is always harmful in the long run!

Suppressed pain will become long-term suffering, which will in turn persist in its hidden life, creating ideal conditions for the onset of an eating disorder.

Thanks to the automatic mechanism of suppressing emotions, you continue living, fully unaware of the existence of any internal suffering. This is why, even after having experienced a "trigger stress", everything may still seem normal.

The hidden, subconscious suffering is constantly active, however, and since its connection to the conscious mind is severed, it sends messages about its existence through other channels – symbolically, through dreams, and physically, expressed as discomfort and fear.

These messages are always from the ego, convincing you of your own worthlessness that will make you unloved and unaccepted.

Faced with these unclear and inexplicable fears, you begin to live in psychological and physical anxiety, creating the feeling of a huge and painful emptiness inside of you.

A lack of faith in your own value then becomes a burden too heavy to carry, extremely intimate and silently present day and night. All along it seems to contradict the real circumstances in your life, which surprises you. Although you feel your life is normal, the anxiety and emptiness deep inside your heart constantly torment and confuse you, because you cannot grasp why they exist and where they are coming from.

Over time, you will begin to notice the absence of some feelings you were sure you had before. The absence of *self-confidence* is what you will notice first. This is followed by a loss of your *trust in life* in general. Soon, you will discover that you cannot feel the *joy of life* or *pleasure* any longer. It feels like life is losing its meaning, turning into anxiety and fear.

A happy life turns into agonizing vegetation.

Caught in the trap of a *whole range of fears*, you are not aware of them until they engulf you. Suddenly, you no longer have a choice and are forced to save yourself immediately. You desperately try to find a way to reduce the anxiety and fill the void within you. You embark on a relentless search for relief and consolation.

An effort to save oneself is always positive and justified, but the attitude you pick for this purpose and begin applying is extremely negative and completely unsuccessful in the long run.

This result is not surprising, because due to your young age and lack of experience, you cannot know that your needs regarding the dysfunctional relationship you had could be met in a healthy and positive manner.

Trying to survive emotionally, you are forced to "break away" from parts of your essence and renounce them. Your only goal is to succeed in the tight "chamber" that threatens to suffocate you.

The rejected parts of you have not disappeared – they just withdraw to the subconscious level. From there, they unsuccessfully wage a war with your ego, confusing you even further. Occasionally, they will flicker in your conscious mind, as a presentiment that something important is missing. Even in those precious moments, you run to bulimia for a solution, which even further suppresses your important needs in life. The more you push your actual needs away, the stronger and more fierce is their return – similar to when you try to hold a large ball deep under water. At the same time as your needs are suppressed, your bulimia grows stronger.

Bulimia is a serious and very powerful disorder, just as the reason that caused it was significant and important. In other words, the ego delivers bulimia as a "solution" to a young woman for all her problems. It then becomes the "justification" for every unwanted or regretted thing she has done in her life, as well as everything she desires, but has not accomplished.

Bulimia as an addiction

Every addiction prohibits personal freedom – a person with an addiction no longer has free will and cannot make decisions freely. This lack of freedom creates suffering and a feeling of emptiness, which is too much for her heart to bear. She is racked with guilt, firmly believing she has nothing. The person then develops an addiction, which calms her down temporarily, helping her forget how much she hates her life and how unhappy she is.

Every activity may become addictive if it has the power to change our mood and make us feel good.

The role of an addiction is to turn our attention away from ourselves, from our real feelings and needs, and especially from painful emotions caused by dysfunctional relationships.

This is why I believe that bulimia is a disease of addiction – an "addiction" to sweet and starchy foods.

In their sensitive teenage years, the only thing that makes emotionally unstable girls happy and comforts them, being always readily available, is *sweet food.*

The wish to quickly eliminate tension is the priority then, and the quickest route proved to be unhealthy – obsessive and addictive – behavior. This is why you took that route without thinking about it first. Food quickly reduced your anxiety, creating a feeling of calm.

And so you would "drug" yourself with sweets, just like adults, for similar reasons, use alcohol, nicotine, or narcotics.

You did not even suspect that it was precisely this behavior that would gradually bring about bulimia.

As a disease, bulimia is characterized precisely by binge eating sweet and fatty foods, as it is only this combination that will produce the desired effect of pleasure.

For all bulimics, binge eating becomes a necessary daily routine, which is the only thing that will mitigate, if only temporarily, the feelings of anxiety and depression that incessantly send signals from the unconscious level.

In doing this, bulimic girls think they have invented and obtained their own "sedatives" and "anxiolytics", which they consider to be harmless.

Due to the real and justified fear of gaining weight as a result of overeating, these smart girls (which they are) think they have also invented a brilliant solution to prevent weight gain. Immediately after overeating, they induce vomiting or, less frequently, use laxatives or excessive exercising, in order to "cleanse" their body of food. In this way they only use what they need – the calming effect of the food, while eliminating the unwanted effects, such as weight gain, by "cleansing". This gives the girls a false feeling of control over their life, whereas they fail to realize that the real issue is actually the avoidance of responsibility.

The bulimic "solution" truly functions perfectly in the beginning. However, girls foolishly disregard the dangerous side effects of bulimia – the development of an addition to carbohydrates, accompanied by numerous metabolic and psychological disorders. They fail to realize that they are being drawn into the vicious circle of bulimia, which pulls them deeper and deeper, without a chance to escape, even once they firmly resolve to do so.

Since personal freedom is a spiritual category, this addiction can only be cured in the spiritual area – by restoring free will and an authentic (positive) identity.

Carbohydrates as "narcotics"

Binge eating foods that are high in carbohydrates works perfectly well for bulimic girls, since it fulfills their need to alleviate painful emotions.

Below is a list of important features of carbohydrates that make them a "bulimic narcotic":

1. *Availability* – food has an advantage of being the only "narcotic" readily available to girls 12 to 15 years old.

2. *Easy integration into the daily routine* – food easily blends into a modern family life with few family meals at the table and works well with normal daily activities of young people, such as studying, socializing, and athletics.

4. *Low price* – sweet foods are cheap, and frequently cost nothing, since most households have a supply of them.

5. *Fast effect* – after only a few minutes, sweet food creates visible pleasure and relief.

6. *Easily concealed addiction* – food addiction can easily remain hidden for a long time, since "overdosing" leaves no immediately visible signs.

"Overdosing" with food in bulimia leaves no permanently visible consequences (in regard to weight gain), as the excessive amount of food is regularly discharged by vomiting.

Every bulimic is constantly obsessed with her appearance, her weight, and the food she eats. It is not uncommon for bulimics to spend hours on end at night in bed thinking about food, planning "feasts" for themselves, and enjoying the images of food in advance. Over time, they lose contact with reality since they are stubbornly determined to fulfill their wishes through the illusion of their addictive bulimic behavior.

Now I would like to discuss another significant issue in bulimia.

Why are bulimic addictive substances exclusively sweet and starchy foods? What is going on with other foods, and why doesn't their overconsumption lead to addiction?

Carbohydrates are the exclusive "narcotic" in bulimia for the simple reason that other types of food, such as salads or fish (vegetables or proteins), do not evoke the desired effect of relaxation and pleasure. Other foods do not have the biochemical ability to change the "chemistry" of the brain in the sense of creating a feeling of pleasure – only carbohydrates can do that.

For substances or activities to become addictive in the first place, they must first fulfill the criteria of creating such changes in the chemistry of the brain, resulting in a "flood" of pleasant physical and psychological emotions.

It is precisely this effect that addictive substances such as narcotics, alcohol, nicotine, or carbohydrates have: they change the chemistry of the brain. These substances have the biochemical ability to "bind" to certain receptors in the brain, increasing the levels of specific chemicals – neurotransmitters (serotonin, dopamine and noradrenaline), creating a strong feeling of pleasure and satisfaction, both psychologically and physically.

So, in many ways bulimia resembles an addiction to alcohol, nicotine, or drugs.

Unfortunately for all addicts, the narcotic feeling of bliss after taking drugs lasts for a relatively short period of time, and as soon as it stops, the addict is again back at square one, back in that well-known state of psychological pain and unfulfilled expectations.

By repeating the same addictive behavior, the memory of the pleasure experienced becomes so strong over time that a desire develops to experience it again.

This leads to the development of a real chemical addiction, a craving that cannot be controlled by free will.

The process of developing an addiction in bulimia is similar that of alcoholics, smokers, and drug addicts, the difference being that an addiction to carbohydrates develops much more slowly.

In bulimia, the addiction is essentially to *sugar*, since all carbohydrates from food, once consumed, turn into the same thing - blood sugar (*glucose*).

With its metabolism, glucose quickly and significantly influences an increase in the level of serotonin in the brain.

Serotonin is a chemical that evokes a strong feeling of satisfaction and calm. These pleasant feelings weaken over time and gradually disappear in bulimic women, due to their fear of weight gain, as the food consumed is forced out of the body by induced vomiting. Serotonin levels in the brain rapidly decrease afterwards. As soon as serotonin levels decrease in the brain, dissatisfaction resurfaces, along with anxiety and uneasiness, a state that a bulimic woman has difficulty handling. Experience teaches her quickly that her unpleasant feelings will go away whenever she wants them to, by another intake of food rich in carbohydrates.

And with her eating binges this is precisely what a bulimic does.

Carbohydrate addiction, like narcotics addiction, progresses over time, becoming more and more severe.

A bulimic's brain will demand ever larger amounts of "carbohydrate drugs" over time, because a *quantity tolerance* slowly begins to develop – i.e. the pleasure decreases with time unless the amount of carbohydrates increases.

As with other addictions, unpleasant withdrawal symptoms develop in bulimia unless the "drug" is administered regularly. Withdrawal symptoms are caused by a chemical imbalance in the bulimic's body, caused by a sudden end to the intake of large amounts of sweet and fatty foods. This chemical imbalance is stronger than any willpower and always wins. In the absence of carbohydrate "drugs", depression, anxiety, and nervousness increase immediately, along with distressing physical states of fatigue, weakness, tremors, and muscle pain. A strong feeling of anxiety is always followed by an overpowering craving for carbohydrates, and every attempt to escape from the bulimic circle of hell is put down by this malignant duo with amazing ease.

Like in other addictions, withdrawal symptoms in bulimia are too strong to be conquered with willpower alone.

The body must be specifically prepared for their elimination, both physically and psychologically. First, the serious chemical imbalance in the body must be restored, and only then can the onset of withdrawal symptoms be prevented, leading the way to a cure as well as a healthy life. This is when preconditions will be met for a return of personal freedom and a search for happiness.

The first precondition for happiness is to be satisfied with yourself. If we seek happiness only elsewhere, in others, we will never attain it. You will not find happiness unless you can love every cell of your body, your breath and your own life. Only this love can make happiness possible; it is real and readily available.

How to discover bulimia

Discovering the "addiction" to carbohydrates is the first step that could lead parents into the right direction.

Detecting whether your daughter, sister, or girlfriend is bulimic is not an easy task. They are obsessively trying to hide their bulimic behavior. I have had patients who were able to hide their addiction from others for as long as seven years and more.

The techniques that bulimics use to hide their addiction are the following:

- they avoid eating with family members, with the excuse that they are not hungry either because they have eaten earlier, or because they are not yet hungry and will eat later;
- when eating with family members, they usually eat a moderate and appropriate cooked meal, and then usually with the excuse that they will clean the kitchen, continue eating whatever they find, sweets in particular, but being very careful that the missing food is not noticed;
- they walk daily "from bakery to bakery", buying sweet pastries and eating them in the street. They repeat this until they overeat, then hurry home or to the nearest bathroom, where they vomit everything eaten. It is not uncommon that, once "empty", they will make another round of the bakeries;
- when they are at home alone, usually in the morning, they plan and embark on a shopping binge, buying huge amounts of their favorite sweets. They bring this food home, and behind a locked door, embarks on a secret "orgy", engaging in recurrent binge eating until all the food is gone;
- they frequently eat at night in their room, carefully hiding the food specifically for this purpose. When they run out of food, they will sneak into the kitchen at night and eat what they can find, replacing the consumed food the next day

so that no one notices, or will make up a story and blame another family member for the missing food;

- at parties they never eat in a normal pattern – they will act in one of two ways: they will either *eat nothing* the entire time and will just drink (oftentimes alcohol) or will take advantage of the bustle and *quickly wolf down some food*, then vomit, and return to overeat again;

- if the party is at their house, they will remain in the kitchen after the guests have left, and with the excuse of cleaning up, they will binge on the leftover sweets;

- they will spend all the money at their disposal (pocket money, money received as a gift) primarily on binge food, or they will steal small, usually unnoticed amounts of money from their parents.

Bulimic girls constantly believe they have found their own formula for slimness and beauty which will impress boys and bring them love. They forget that boys today are not naive, and that they are more observant and understanding than the boys of earlier generations.

I was quite surprised myself by my neighbor's twenty-year-old son, who was told on one occasion that there are more and more beautiful girls looking like models, and that he should find one for himself. His answer was: "I am sick of them! There are pretty girls everywhere, but when I see slim girls eating and drinking like they work in a mine, I know something is wrong. They must be bulimic."

"Well, look at that, modern boys have made things quite simple," I thought, impressed with his accurate observation.

Although methods of hiding bulimic binges are quite efficient and cunning, parents should not have a hard time discovering whether their daughter is bulimic or not, if they take the right steps.

Parents can make an accurate diagnosis when they manage, unnoticed, to note the number, amounts, and contents of their daughter's daily meals.

It is important to gradually eliminate, or significantly reduce, the amount of sweets and snacks in the house, and to keep precise track of food supplies in the house.

Try to discover, without her knowing, whether your daughter is hiding cookies, snacks, and chocolate supplies in her room.

Noting the amount of money available, both yours and hers, is crucial on a daily basis, since a bulimic, forced by her addiction, must spend significant amounts of money on food every day.

If you notice several warning signs after 2 to 3 weeks of monitoring, turn your attention to the most significant one – an obvious discrepancy between excessive meals and her low weight.

If all the signs are there, you can determine with great certainty that your daughter has bulimia.

This must be followed by a serious and important talk, where you should remove all her defenses and, with consideration and understanding, get to the truth. Then offer her your understanding and unconditional love: you must accept reality and show her you are ready to provide her with all the help and support that is necessary.

Bulimic overeating

In relation to other addictions, the hardest addiction to discover is the overeating of carbohydrates and fatty foods.

It is typical, especially in early stages of the disease, that bulimics are not aware of their addiction at all, since it is mixed with their usual behavior and a vital physiological need. Everyone in the world must eat every day, which is why it is hard to assess whether a person's eating is an addiction or a regular pattern within normal limits. However, the addict herself may easily recognize when her eating is addictive, because it will have specific characteristics.

Addictive eating is characterized by the following:
- a special type of *anxiety*, inseparable from an *overpowering craving* for sweet food;
- a constant *feeling of hunger*, regardless of whether the stomach is full or not;
- an inability to feel real physiological hunger due to a constantly present craving for food;
- complete loss of control over the amount of food consumed – addictive eaters continue eating until their stomach is overfilled and they feel nauseous;
- an overly intense, almost hypnotic feeling of *bliss and pleasure* when eating;
- a strong connection between craving sweet foods and the onset of strong emotions, mostly negative, such as self-hatred, depression, disappointment, despair, sorrow, and the like.

Addictive binge eating may co-occur with strong positive emotions as well, when bulimics are praised, successful, or recognized. In these circumstances, the trigger for binge eating is the addict's confusion with happiness in unusual, positive situations (as they are only used to depression).

After eating binges, "drugged" with sweet food, an anxious and nervous girl quickly becomes calm and full. By regularly repeating binges, she begins to notice that only overeating can mitigate and her fears, concerns, and stresses, making them bearable, especially since this also gives her moments of intense pleasure. Unfortunately, she fails to realize that she is falling unintentionally into the trap of addiction to carbohydrates, becoming a captive of the bulimic way of life.

Both the girl and her parents must understand that an addictive craving for carbohydrates is so strong that a bulimic cannot control it with her own free will.

The exhausting bulimic lifestyle has its better days, when girls invest great effort and willpower to stop the binge eating and live a healthy life. However, after a short initial success, her previous emotional patterns will easily surface with the next subsequent stressful situation, which will pull her back into the disease with even stronger intensity.

If the addict attempts self-healing by completely omitting carbohydrates from her diet, her craving for carbohydrates, along with her addiction, will become more intense over time. When carbohydrates are completely omitted from the diet for longer than a month, the craving explodes during the next stressful situation, especially if it is an emotional one. The addict will have to fulfill this craving for carbohydrates immediately with even more intense recurrent binge eating. This is why individual attempts at healing fail instantly.

And this is why I stress that the only real way to overcome bulimia is through professional – medical, nutritionist, and psychotherapeutic – help.

First, it is necessary to reestablish a biochemical balance in the metabolism, so that the addictive craving for carbohydrates does not reoccur!

It is only when the craving disappears on its own that the bulimic will stop thinking about it and forget that it ever existed.

The addiction to carbohydrates will then cease to be an issue in her life, just as the non-smoker never craves a cigarette, since smoking is simply not an issue for him.

A rebalanced metabolism will function normally forever, on the condition that carbohydrates are consumed regularly, on a daily basis. However, these carbohydrates will be completely different – with a low glycemic index. I will discuss this in more detail in the chapter on creating a dietary program.

The stages of developing bulimia

Like in other addictions, pleasure is increasingly hard to achieve in bulimia after a period of time, regardless of the amount of carbohydrates consumed. Bulimics then enter a new, more difficult and more dangerous stage. They do not engage in binge eating for pleasure, but to avoid the unpleasant withdrawal symptoms. In this stage of the addiction, all pleasure disappears, since the young woman is primarily trying to escape from her symptoms of anxiety, nervousness, and depression. All she does is submissively feed her addiction – her powerful "master".

The onset of this stage is proof that her case bulimia developed a long time ago, some five years earlier, and that over time it has become stable and established.

In such circumstances I am fully aware that bulimia has completely infiltrated the life and behavior of the patient, and that her chances for recovery are much lower than in earlier stages of the disease.

However, in such advanced stages of bulimia, I have occasionally noticed a paradox that often helped in treatment. When a seriously sick young woman realizes her helplessness in the addiction, becomes aware that her life revolves exclusively around overeating and vomiting, and realizes that her personality has become revoltingly unrecognizable – in other words, when she hits rock bottom – her life with bulimia may repulse her so much that it leads to an unbelievably strong determination to fight it, one that sees no limits. She truly becomes a "warrior" at this point, ready to find her "authentic self" again, whatever the cost.

The only thing she says then is this: "Please, tell me what I must do to get better. I will do everything, even if my life is at stake."

I ask her to remember the authentic and spontaneous person she once was, so that, with my help, instructions, and explanations, she might finally realize with clarity how unnecessary and naive she was when she embarked on her bulimic adventure.

At this point, the girl usually turns to her parents, opens up, and admits her problem.

Only then does she become ready for treatment.

The parents usually realize how serious the situation is only at this point, and finally cease with their useless complaints and criticism. They join their parental energy, love, and patience to begin helping their child to overcome the problem.

This phenomenon has helped me achieve rapid progress in a number of situations, even full recovery, especially in cases where bulimia was severe and had lasted a long time – as much as ten years.

Joining forces, the parents, the girl, and I would then succeed in forcing bulimia to its knees once we had pulled the victim away from it, defending her with an entire "army" led by knowledge and love.

On the other hand, girls with only a short history of bulimia often are not sure whether they want to change their bulimic lifestyle, since it has enabled them to achieve easily their goal of staying slim. They come to therapy against their will, primarily because their parents have discovered their bulimic behavior and, alarmed, made them seek therapy.

In these cases everything depends on the knowledge and experience of the physician. If the physician succeeds in explaining the danger that further development of the disease poses to the girl, and if he manages to convince her that there are other – healthier and easier – ways of accomplishing goals in life, then the therapy has a chance of success.

PART FOUR
THE SCHOOL OF POSITIVE THINKING

Regaining your health

When discussing how to regain your health, I always fully rely on the following:
- your genuine desire to get well,
- your honest cooperation,
- your intelligence,
- your (remaining) common sense,
- your (remaining) logic,
- your (remaining) strength,
- your (remaining) patience,
- your exceptional intuition,
- your readiness to learn about life,
- your need to live without fear,
- your readiness to work on yourself,
- your need for a positive change,
- your need for calm and happiness,
- your need to make peace with yourself,
- your need to come to terms with your own life,
- your need for unconditional love,
- your need to trust life in general,

and finally, most importantly, I count on your being truly disgusted with the fact that your bulimic ego is running your life, and that you have finally said "ENOUGH"!

I will need all this, because the change you desire demands complete dedication for you to reach the goal of health and happiness, as well as a strong determination to attain that goal.

If you fulfill at least seven of the above-listed expectations, your chances of success are excellent!

To fully succeed, you must all become "warriors", building a force that is fearless of the "enemy" and its obstacles, that doesn't retreat when circumstances demand that you stand steady and persevere, moving steadily forward with enthusiasm, celebrating your newly found freedom.

Overcoming bulimia will begin for each one of you once you are capable of clearly understanding all the misery and uselessness of your bulimic patterns, and admit having taken the wrong path, which has taken you further away from, not closer to, your desired goals.

You must have jealously looked at girls on magazine covers more times than you can count - slim, perfect beauties, clearly happy with themselves. You could not understand how they did it. They seemed spontaneous and relaxed, as if the fact that they were famous and successful was the most natural thing in the world. It seemed as if they had a code for happiness that for some reason remained inaccessible to you. You envied them because of your inferiority complexes, truly convinced that it was unfair that life had chosen and rewarded them and not you, without any effort or merit on their part. While they simply glided through their fantasy-like lives, you had to invest huge efforts and fight hard for every success. That is why you feel so betrayed today, as if life has forgotten you and passed you by.

Believe me, all such thoughts are nothing more than products of your own mind, reacting to the superficial trends of an equally confused environment. You have accepted every seemingly reasonable thought from your surroundings, over time creating your own conviction about the truth, based solely on these statements, without a reality check.

In fact, the truth is something completely different.

Neither are other girls perfectly beautiful and happy, nor are you ugly and shunned.

The only person who betrayed you is you yourself; You abandoned real life while innocently assuming a false one, only because it was presented in colorful wrapping that you liked.

I believe you finally realize now that the things you think about constantly and are focused on incessantly become your convictions over time.

Likewise, when you believe in something for a time, it convinces you that this is the truth. When you truly believe something, it becomes your *rule of life*. With its mutual force of belief, emotions, and behavior, this rule of life will always write an identical *life's script* for you, bringing about the same *results in life*.

You entirely trusted your mind - incessantly devising your own "brilliant" strategies for success. You fully trusted your own thoughts, unaware that your negative and vain ego was involved as well. Instead of being your loyal servant, your egoistic thoughts became your dictator and only master. This is how you unintentionally created your own "monster", seeming to save you, but in fact destroying you over the long term.

Your double-faced ego would tempt you with its whisper, convince you with ease, flatter and paint beautiful castles in the sky. Soon after, it would scare you with terrible failures, tempt you with delusions and drive you crazy with appealing new promises.

One of your ego's cunning ideas, which you believed blindly, was the "brilliant" idea of a bulimic lifestyle.

Only after you "wake up" from your egoistic, bulimic dream,

having become fully aware of your own false beliefs and misconceptions, will you be ready to eliminate the bulimic limitations from your life.

I am offering this "wake-up call" in the school of positive thinking.

Steps leading to health

In order to overcome bulimia yourself, you have to complete the following seven steps:

Step one
Once you have *analyzed* your own bulimic convictions and experiences in detail, you must realize and strongly feel that this lifestyle has no positive value or prospects for you whatsoever.

Step two
When your detailed analysis is complete, you must truly recognize, discover, and analyze your *naive youthful convictions* (which led you down the road to bulimia in the first place). Only then will you be able to renounce them as false, without regret or hesitation.

This is how you become *aware of their falsity* and your own misconceptions.

Step three
Once you realize the absurdity of your perception of life based on your bulimic ego, you must reach a *conscious and determined decision* to change all your false convictions about yourself and your life.

Step four
This is the most important step. Now you are ready to find out, recognize, learn, and accept something *new*.
I will teach you about *natural spiritual laws*, in the light of which you will see *important truths about life*, and experience them in a new and essentially different manner.
Your current image of your existing life, filled with misconceptions, will become fully clear to you, enabling you to forgive yourself for your ignorance.

Step five
This is the point where you are approaching a decisive move.
By accepting and using your *new knowledge*, you will spontaneously create an adequate *new, positive perception of life*.
Your new attitudes will initiate desired changes on their own with their positive energy.

Step six
This is the decisive step.
With your new perception of life, you must *overcome* and transform your existing negative *emotions*, so that they begin *cooperating* harmoniously with the ongoing change.
Emotions are the most significant link, harmonizing and changing the flow of energy in the body's cells. This is why *they are decisive* for harmony or disharmony, depending on their nature.
Emotions are critically important, as they are the ones exclusively initiating changes in behavior, which will in turn affect your accomplishments in life.

Step seven
The result of new knowledge, new positive attitudes, and new

positive emotions will be a new, positive feeling about life. It will spontaneously bring about more positive and practical behavior. This behavior will result in a completely new, *modified physical reaction*, returning the *metabolism*, out of balance in bulimia, to its normal state, and the craving to overeat, along with the desire to induce vomiting, will disappear. Along with a balanced diet and moderate exercise, this will enable your body to burn excessive fat and shape its muscles, without you having to invest a special effort or struggle.

The conclusion is clear: the essence of the desired change lies in your new convictions and feelings, not in actions alone.

The desired behavior will set in spontaneously, as an automatic side effect of the emotions you bring about with your new knowledge and intentional, focused (but this time positive) thoughts!

Training your thoughts and emotions

Understand your emotions instead of feeding them!
Your *convictions*, the thoughts you absolutely trust, are the ones making exclusive decisions about your life.
The convictions that dominate are the ones which are *stronger* in a certain situation, regardless of whether they are conscious or not.
Although every bulimic has a number of good intentions and desires, she will not, unfortunately, make decisions about the quality of her life. This will be done by her deeply negative convictions (about her own worthlessness) that she has mistaken for truth in difficult moments of her childhood.
I have to emphasize the *immense power and influence of*

subconscious negative convictions, since they developed a long time ago and are now set in stone. These convictions influence all your daily thoughts with their *basic negative aspect*.

Since convictions produce identical emotions, your *subconscious negative convictions* have been creating identical negative and unpleasant emotions for years. They can only be transformed into desired, positive ones by new, positive convictions. The latter will succeed only once they are *stronger than the previous*, subconscious ones. This is the only way to transform previous, negative emotions into positive ones.

New, positive emotions will immediately result in positive changes in behavior, which will ultimately result in the desired goal, overcoming bulimia.

When applying this Program, you will see it for yourselves: as soon as you *succeed in changing* your negative thoughts and convictions into positive ones, your overwhelming craving for carbohydrates will stop on its own!

To achieve this it is necessary to attain a *new perception of life* that is strong and inspiring enough to overcome your previous, subconscious negative convictions.

The hardest part of all is to change one's previous, negative convictions about oneself, both conscious and unconscious. It is essential to modify the overall train of thought about oneself and one's values, until one's thoughts become purely positive, as nature intended them in the first place.

All people who have some serious problem in their lives that remains unresolved for a long time (including everyone suffering from eating disorders) *have an automatic negative attitude toward this problem.*

Like everything else, your choice of food is a result of your convictions – more unconscious than conscious ones – that developed, settled and became deeply rooted in you over a period of time in the past. This is why your reactions are automatic, although it all boils down to the process of automatic thought, a repetitive pattern which created your automatic mental habit.

Your mental habit will spontaneously produce consistently identical automatic emotions. In other words, whenever you have a negative experience, you believe and consider it to be negative (having made up your mind about this a long time ago), you immediately begin to feel badly. This feeling spontaneously creates negative behavior – in the case of bulimia, this is the craving to overeat sweet food and induce vomiting.

All the problems in your life will continue unresolved precisely due to your powerful negative convictions about these problems, convictions acquired in your childhood and early adulthood and which are deeply rooted in your subconscious mind.

Can you understand how pathetic you have become – with your automatic thoughts, feelings, and reactions, the worst being that you are not even aware of them? Likewise, you are also unaware of the possibility of change, not having given it the attention it deserves.

Your subconscious mind is not doing anything special – it contains a number of previous perceptions of life that have been stored along the way, and for the most part negative, false ones. It is the subconscious mind, nothing else, that runs your life now, always in the same defeating manner.

The most important thing to bear in mind is that your *emotions* (including your spontaneous behavior) will *always resemble your deepest (and therefore strongest) convictions.*

All convictions you have about yourself today, in bulimia's

grip, come from the subconscious mind, which means they stem from your past and are exceptionally negative, revealing a pattern of fear and lack of faith in yourself.

A transformation from unwanted forms of behavior to desired ones was previously not possible precisely because a strong opposing conviction was in your subconscious mind – that this change is too hard and thus impossible for you. This limiting, subconscious conviction was always stronger than your conscious desires and attempts, and its victory was therefore easy.

But things do not have to stay this way!

If you truly want to change your (bulimic) behavior with all your heart, you must first change your essential perceptions of life from negative to positive ones. This can happen once you adopt new perceptions about life, which I will explain in detail later in the book.

Harmonizing your emotions with your new, positive convictions will not be easy, so arm yourself with patience. Emotions are essential in the process of change.

Your existing negative emotions will be transformed into positive ones only when your new, positive perception of life overpowers the previous, negative emotions from your subconscious mind.

Strong and fully positive thoughts have the power to permeate and transform your entire personality, spontaneously evoking equally strong positive emotions of love, joy, trust, and enthusiasm. If your emotions become this positive, your entire life will as well.

In your mind you will begin to foster only happy thoughts, filled with love. When these thoughts turn into strong, determined positive emotions and attitudes, these wonderful positive emotions in turn will automatically create preconditions for the life you want.

Since emotions determine behavior, your newly created positive emotions will immediately harvest positive results through different, spontaneously positive behavior.

In addition, everything else will change spontaneously as well, without strenuous effort:

- you will regain your former self-confidence,
- you will become calm and have peace of mind,
- you will be optimistic and enthusiastic,
- your diet will consist of new, healthy foods,
- your relationships with others will take on a new dimension – you will understand them better and will be able to forgive them,
- your metabolic balance will be reestablished, and your body will function properly again.

The result of all these changes will be *health and happiness*.

New thoughts – new convictions

Thoughts are essential, everything starts with them.

We have *direct control* only over our thoughts, since we can choose our thoughts as we want to. We do this all the time, consciously or not, and select our thoughts according to the level of our maturity, life experience, and knowledge we possess.

Negative thoughts (fear, worries, bitterness) are disease for the soul. They lead to unpleasant feelings and moods, which in turn result in bad decisions (in bulimia – binge eating). Frequent bad decisions over a period of time result in physical illness.

It is important to think about your motivating, positive goals with absolute faith in success, and to frequently visualize them with a feeling of joy – this road leads to the fulfillment of wishes whereby you will live your life as an authentic person. No masks or feigning happiness will be necessary then.

The easiest and correct solution is to focus, with positive thoughts, on the present moment, on life here and now – on what you are eating, drinking, or doing at this moment or on what you are thinking about. This is the only thing you do control.

By using this method, directing your thoughts toward positive thinking, you will succeed in mastering your emotions, transforming negative emotions into positive ones, and making your emotions work for you. Your body will accept your thoughts and follow through in terms of health.

Here are some examples of this.

Example I
What happens if you wake up on a beautiful morning with the thought that it would do you well to go for a jog by the river and get some fresh air?

Completely different actions can develop from this thought, depending on your convictions and resulting emotions, which will surface spontaneously to *specify* which convictions are true and should be taken into consideration.

First outcome: If spontaneous emotions of a pleasant excitement and happy expectations are evoked when thinking about jogging by the river, then these emotions will realize your thoughts easily, and make your body work out.

This means that no conflict between your wishes and your convictions has occurred, and that your convictions are positive in regard to this topic.

What happens always happens here – spontaneous emotions in

harmony with the existing positive convictions have occurred, resulting in your engaging in the desired activity.

Second outcome: If you have the same thought but do not succeed in getting your emotions on board, you will end up with feelings of boredom and anxiety. You will surely not go for a jog in this case, but will look for pleasure in the usual places – in front of a TV, for example.

Why does this happen when your thoughts, desire, and positive intention were all there?

Aware that physical activity is healthy, you truly wanted to go jogging.

So where did the feeling of resistance due to which your body refused to jog come from?

Why did your body sabotage its own wishes and good intentions?

It happened because something stronger than your wishes and desires dragged you back into passivity.

You failed to accomplish the desired activity because you didn't succeed in evoking the necessary emotions with your thoughts. Your emotions remained the same as before, since they are *still at the mercy of someone else – more powerful thoughts and convictions* – that you are fully unaware of. This is your previous, usual way of thinking, which dominates your subconscious mind in the form of a strong conviction that exercise is hard and boring.

You have adopted this conviction as the truth through an event in the past, perhaps already forgotten, that was probably reestablished several times, turning into a strong subconscious conviction with an intense and secret force that ultimately always shapes reality.

Example II
A mother, whose small child ran in front of a car and was crushed by it, managed to lift the part of the excessively heavy vehicle (which she would not have been able to move at all under normal circumstances) to free her child. In these situations there is no time for thinking. The mother's *conviction* that she was responsible for the life of her child, fully rooted in her deepest subconscious mind, through the strongest *emotion* of all – maternal love – spontaneously and instantly produced an amazingly strong physical reaction (*conduct*), the only adequate one for this situation, measurable only with the emotion that produced it.

These examples show that emotions are of essential importance, being the main mediator between convictions and behavior, always reflecting only the real (not desired) convictions.

Subconscious convictions determine your overall behavior, and consequently, your life, but because they have been hidden by your mind and consciousness, you cannot reach them. This means you have no clue about what you *really* think and *truly* believe in.
Emotions are therefore a very practical tool for recognizing your own subconscious convictions that determine your life! Whatever you think about and whatever you desire, emotions that surface spontaneously will *precisely indicate your true convictions* about a certain topic, which will make your supporting actions much clearer.

Previous convictions are almost always stronger than new ones, since they have been around for a while and have thus been strengthened. This is why our emotions always surrender to previous, familiar convictions rather than to new and different ones.

It is important to remember that all the significant, usual emotions we feel daily were created with the power of our subconscious convictions from the past.

In other words, although we can choose the positive or negative nature of our thoughts, the emotions that surface along with these thoughts have absolute executive force, and only they determine our actual behavior and actions.

Negative convictions produce identical negative emotions, and negative emotions produce only negative behavior. Numerous subconscious convictions of this kind are responsible for the onset of bulimia.

This is why it is so extremely difficult to change deep-rooted negative behavior patterns that have become habits.

Example III

An excellent example of the absolute power that subconscious convictions have is the failure of bulimics to stop their overeating rituals and induced vomiting, even when they want to stop.

Their conscious, positive thoughts will always be defeated easily by their previous, negative, subconscious convictions, since they dominate emotions in bulimia, which also determine (bulimic) behavior.

The subconscious convictions of bulimics, formed in childhood or in early adulthood, are mostly negative, in line with negative thinking process and life experiences of young people during the turbulent years of puberty and adolescence.

Since all bulimics are individuals with exceptionally negative perceptions of life (mental attitudes), all their emotions will be negative as well, a state which invariably results in a failed and miserable life.

Two main conclusions can be drawn from the above:
1. Every person will behave the way they feel, and feel the way their conscious and (especially) unconscious beliefs have taught them to over the years.

2. None of us is aware of what all our convictions are, collected from birth on, and how they have determined our lives, since we have no conscious knowledge of the convictions dominating our emotions throughout our lives.

These conclusions provide a new understanding of our lives until the present moment. Additionally, they offer a breakthrough solution as well. They allow us to analyze and establish which convictions, positive or negative, determine our lives in different situations.

We can do this by simply asking ourselves *how exactly we feel* at a certain moment or in regard to a problem.

By recognizing the nature, intensity, and significance of every emotion connected to a certain situation, we are able to identify our positive or negative convictions in each situation.

When we recognize the feelings of anxiety and fear, we will know that a very negative conviction is dominating in that situation, where such convictions primarily stem from the subconscious mind and have usually been present in our lives for a while.

On the other hand, if we feel happiness and pleasure in the same situation, we will be able to identify our positive convictions about this topic, aware that our behavior is on the right track as well.

Important rule of life:
A positive perception of life (an optimistic attitude) attracts positive emotions and healthy behavior in our life, while

negative perceptions (pessimistic attitudes) always attract negative emotions and unhealthy behavior.

Your success in everything you do does not depend on luck and coincidence, but exclusively on your mental attitude about life.

A mental attitude is a set of all the convictions you have about your own life and life in general. You reach decisions, make assessments and engage in all your activities based on it.

Your life will depend on your mental attitude.

Your mental attitude is usually UNCONSCIOUS, however the sum of all the convictions you have gathered in life up to this point should be a CONSCIOUS one – focused and programmed by your present mind, to accomplish your present wishes, plans, and decisions.

Not many people realize how defeating and painful a person's life can be when they are controlled by wrong and false convictions that they accumulated in their subconscious mind in childhood. In your innocent childhood years you believed everyone around you. And there must have been enough people and events in your childhood and in school, to convince you that you are not good enough, beautiful enough, or worthy enough of love.

And so you have lived your life with the burdens of distrusting yourself and your values, burdens that were too heavy to carry. Convictions can be dangerous.

They get very deeply and strongly rooted and dominate the brain which stops being objective.

And unconsciously, spontaneously, regardless of your age, you continue to perceive and experience your whole life through the eyes of the anxious child that you once were.

Instead of turning your life in a positive direction with your adult mind, you continue to live the defeatist lifestyle you learned and adopted in childhood and in early adulthood.

You must always be aware of the fact that you have direct and full control only *in choosing your thoughts* to focus on.

It is precisely this possibility of the *freedom to think* that provides a valuable opportunity for us all to plan our lives and create a life we want.

Therefore, if you want to change your present behavior and your current lifestyle, the first step is to begin thinking in a completely different, fully positive way.

A solution works in two ways: your convictions always predict the same type of emotion and behavior that will resurface, just like every behavior always indicates which convictions dominate – positive or negative ones.

Every person becomes precisely the image of her thoughts and convictions!

Only after you fully understand and apply this, will it become possible to change your undesired behavior and habits.

The road to awareness

I will now take you on an important "journey".

Our trip will be the discovery of the path in life that will bring you to your desired goal – the joy of authentic existence.

If you manage to understand the signs along the way and remain determined in your wishes and determination, you will activate your sleepy consciousness and overcome bulimia, finally reaching your goal – health.

It took me 30 years to discover, understand, and walk this path. I walked slowly, paving the way myself. You will go faster, because I will show you some shortcuts, give you a push on steep inclines, and offer my hand on bridges. When we reach our goal, the formula for a healthy and happy existence will be forever yours.

This path, like a time machine, takes you away from the past. It is an exit from the "prison-castle" that was created during your childhood with the aim of protection, "constructed" to help you recover from pain that you had suffered. Its thick walls truly played their part – protecting you from new "blows" but distancing you from real life.

After years of "hiding in the castle," you are no longer aware that this protection exists. It has remained active in your subconscious, masked and well hidden from your conscious mind. This is why you are unaware that you have been a prisoner of your own self for years. Your "true self" remained locked in the "castle", while your masks had freedom, skillfully adapting to different situations and needs.

You fail to realize you are living like split personalities – one an unhappy, trapped girl, and the other a grown, damaged young woman, attempting in vain to live a reasonable and successful life. This is why you have felt strange and unreal for years, as if you were several walking puppets or "zombies", unsure whether and why you were alive at all.

The secret lies in the fact that the childhood "castle" and the lonely girl in it have been secret masters of your life all along. The girl is still lonely, scared, and desperate. She is hungry for love, and trusts no one. She sends these feelings to her body day and night, hiding from your conscious mind. And so your body has its own sick, independent life in bulimia, stubbornly refusing to cooperate with your wishes and desires. You feel completely distant from them, which makes you anxious and helpless.

You have attempted to change this horrific feeling of being like a puppet more times than you can count. You have used all your willpower to force yourself to live a life you perceived as healthy and right, but to no avail. All along, you felt like a person rowing upstream on a fast river. The more you forced yourself to make a positive change, the more your body seemed to snicker at you, continuing to behave as it wished.

After tremendous effort, the same thing happened over and over again – you were forced to give up and return into bulimia's grip. The "adult you" persisted in putting on one of your many masks, continuing to feign normal life.

For a moment, try to imagine yourself as that little girl, enclosed in a castle. Try to feel her immense wish to escape.

Imagine the walls in this prison-castle being made of firm, nonstretchable rubber. Imagine yourself – the little girl – pushing at the heavy door, trying to break out, having lost the key a long time ago, running into walls, trying to escape, and desperately looking for an exit.

The rubber walls, like an extended slingshot, always push her back, with the same force as hers. The harder she tries, and the more she pushes, the stronger the resistance.

Now you realize that, with her force and the walls' resistance, she had no chance.

The reason is that she tried to remove the walls only with the power of her will and the force of her suffering. The force she used hit her right back, like a boomerang. She remained equally desperate as she had been in the beginning.

Every subsequent attempt made her less ready to fight, with an increasing fear of failure. She sought change solely through her despair, unaware that the strength of calm and happiness can accomplish so much more.

The nature of an action always determines an equivalent reaction. And precisely because of this, she was unable to become happy, due to her immense fear.

Once you understand that this scared girl still determines your feelings and your entire life, you will realize why all your attempts to cure yourself were doomed to fail from the start.

Do you realize now that well-being cannot be accomplished through fear and forcing yourself to fight and suffer, but only through something completely different?

For your life to change the way you want it to, the "girl" in you must see it in a different light, think about it differently, and fully trust her new thoughts.

The solution lies in her completely new, positive feeling about life and her place in it, as well as in a determined belief in this positive attitude. Only then will her feelings spontaneously transform into joy and trust, and as such will permeate every cell of her body. New messages from your subconscious mind will overwrite previous ones, providing you with "adult" consciousness, health, and peace.

Rules for a happy life

The most important issue in overcoming bulimia should be the following:

How will we manage to develop positive thinking and positive convictions in order to generate the new pattern of behavior that we desire?

My answer is: *with new knowledge about the rules for a happy life!*

The more you learn and discover, the better your thoughts will be shaped, which will help you develop stronger and more positive convictions.

You will not doubt these thoughts; they will be confirmed by your knowledge, convictions, and experience, and not like previously, with imposed and unverified ideas imposed by others, which you mistook for the truth in your childhood, as you lacked both knowledge and experience.

You have never selected your thoughts consciously before – i.e. with your willpower and intention – but only filtered and kept the messages that were heard, seen, or imposed by the outside world. A good example of this is countless number of aggressive marketing images and messages on television and in magazines. Such a subconscious way of thinking is still undesirable, as it is mostly negative.

It is necessary for you to be conscious of your thoughts and to try and reject all unnecessary, negative, and unverified ones. You must always bear in mind that the only thoughts, wishes, and ideas that matter and come true are those which you truly believe in, regardless of whether you want to believe them or not.

This *new knowledge* will help you to develop positive convictions, and desired emotions will follow. These positive emotions will then spontaneously direct you to new, correct behavior, which will ultimately result in healthy physical reactions and desired goals in life.

In other words, if you want to live a new and happy life, you must first transform into a new and happy person.

"Sure, but how?"

"By teaching yourselves to produce happy emotions!"

"Teach us fast! How do we do that?"

"Simply – by becoming aware of the real truth about life, a truth that brings peace and happiness and releases you from pain forever. When you realize your true value and how precious your life is, you will shine with your feelings of security and love. Once you trust your new thoughts completely, success is guaranteed!

Your new, positive convictions will release positive emotions, which will then spontaneously produce the new, desired form of behavior."

Feel the rhythm of nature

Remember, for instance, how difficult it is to reverse the course of negative thinking when the first negative thought appears, because one leads to another, creating a negative mood which is static and hard to change.

Happy thoughts follow a similar pattern; they simply attach themselves to one another and produce cheerful and enthusiastic moods.

When the thoughts and the body are harmonious, they have one single rhythm, attracting one another.

The vibration of the *directed thoughts* we believe in may influence our body by gradually changing the vibration of its cells in the process of harmonization, until they are ultimately in sync with our thoughts.

This means that our daily thoughts and the convictions that result from them influence our physical bodies constantly, making them adapt or gradually change, precisely in accordance with the nature of our convictions. We do this all the time, usually subconsciously and unintentionally, unaware that it affects the way our body will act. An example of this is a psychosomatic disorder (psychos = psyche, soma = body), in which a physical disease is preceded by a long period of a negative psychological state.

Example – when a person directs repulsive, intolerant and hateful thoughts to her body over a long period of time, the strong negative energy of these thoughts will force the body to vibrate to the same negative rhythm, keeping the body precisely in an undesired state, and preventing any change for the better.

The opposite is true as well – when someone simply accepts and loves their body the way it is, the positive energy of this train of thought will continually harmonize their body until it becomes healthy and strong.

So our body always reflects the thoughts and convictions we have about it.

Every wish is a certain vibration as well.

Whether a certain wish will be realized or will remain a wish only depends solely on your true conviction regarding this wish.

The possibility of every wish being fulfilled will best predict the emerging emotions, as they spontaneously reflect only your true convictions, which you may not be aware of at times.

The strength and nature of the emotions evoked will indicate precisely and exactly the strength of your belief in a thought or its realization!

Every wish you have will result in one of two scenarios:

Scenario in which a wish is fulfilled: if you feel relaxed, self-confident, and calm in regard to a certain wish, this indicates your positive and strong faith in it. Be patient and your wish will certainly come true.

Scenario in which a wish is not fulfilled: the process is completely different if you are focused on a wish, *wanting to believe* it will be fulfilled, but deep inside *not believing it.* Anxiety and nervousness develop, accompanied by fear and doubt, and this must be an immediate indicator of what your real conviction is regarding that wish. Naturally, the negative emotions that are present will immediately reveal the truth – that your actual belief in this wish is nonexistent. The *strength* of this negative conviction will be clear from your emotions regarding this wish – they will be extremely *negative (anxiety, fear, doubt)*.

That your *actual belief* is negative, stemming from your subconscious mind and the past, will be immediately clear as soon as you recognize that your emotions are negative, since this means they have not followed the positive attempts made by your mind and willpower.

The vibration of these negative emotions will result in a real situation turning out exactly as you feared – the opposite of what you wished for.

This second scenario is often present in your wish to lose weight, since it encompasses *two conflicting convictions – a false one* (a positive wish) *and a real one* (a negative subconscious conviction).

A good example of this is the e-mail below from Petra, one of countless that I have received:

> Dear Doctor Skoro, please help me!
> I am 20 years old and am studying economics in Zagreb. I am 168 cm tall and weigh 75 kg. I desperately want to lose 10 kg, but have always been horrified by exercise and diets. I am constantly tormented by my weight and have been obsessing about losing weight for weeks. I have become moody and depressed, I hate my body, and the strangest part is that although I think about losing weight all the time, it only makes me hungrier. Instead of watching what I eat, I find myself constantly nibbling on the foods I should not be eating - chocolate, cookies, cake, pastries...

To make matters worse, I have not moved from my couch for days, the TV is constantly on, I have stopped studying, and all of a sudden, I find all the shows interesting.

I am very mad at myself and my behavior!

My desire to lose weight is growing, but no matter how hard I try, I cannot make myself do anything about it.

I am feeling worse by the day, since the scale is showing bigger numbers, instead of smaller ones.

I cannot understand why my behavior is persistently the opposite of what I want.

Why do I sabotage myself?

Why am I unable to lose weight?

Please, help me. Thank you in advance.

Desperate Petra

Here is my answer:

Dear Petra,

You are a typical girl who believes that problems can and must be solved only with your desire and wish to change them. Unfortunately, reality is proving you wrong, hinting that there are other important "players" in this game.

Your problem is that there is a conflict between your *wishes* and your convictions.

Your *emotions* created spontaneously in this conflict will always decide on the victory, and they will always reflect your real convictions.

In other words, the master of all *wishes* and thoughts that *always come true* is the real, unquestionable conviction or *belief.*

Your unhealthy obsession with weight is in fact a very strong negative thought, reflected in equally strong negative emotions of despair, fear, and doubt. These negative emotions have directly produced what else but equally negative behavior – overeating – resulting in a negative physical reaction – weight gain.

Deep inside, you did not believe in success from the start, as you have admitted that you hate exercising and dieting. Your lack of faith in success was reflected in identical negative vibrations, indicating your real convictions, or in your case – *non-convictions*.

Your thoughts (wishes), as a product of your willpower, were thus immediately defeated, having been superficial, more an *attempt to believe* than actually believing. As such, they did not match your real convictions about the topic.

I hope you finally realize that your real conviction (belief) in the possibility of losing weight has been around for a long time, deeply rooted in your subconscious mind, and was absolutely negative. You had created it in the past, confirming it during every previous attempt to lose weight. The fact that this conviction is subconscious means that it is hidden from your conscious mind, and explains why you are unaware of its existence. Your emotions are subject to these convictions, without you being aware of them at all. Negative emotions had then produced automatic negative behavior, and that is where your negative outcome comes from.

Subconscious convictions always come true, being long-term, dominant, and decisive. Unfortunately, they are always negative, having been created in stressful and unfavorable situations in your childhood, puberty, or adolescence. These actual negative convictions regarding the possibility of losing weight have easily dominated your wish to lose weight, as there is no true belief behind it.

On the other hand, your real – negative – convictions produced equally negative emotions (self-hatred, anxiety, depression, and hunger), which in turn created negative behavior (physical inactivity, overeating) that not only prevented the loss of weight, but actually resulted in weight gain.

How can you solve your problem then?

The solution is as follows:

You must create a new, positive conviction to dominate the previous, negative one!

Your new conviction can arise only from new knowledge, or through the creation of new, different, positive attitudes in life. You must stop thinking about the topics of weight gain and weight loss, because you have bad experiences and have established negative convictions. You must turn to those positive attitudes in life which you have never doubted.

This will get you on the right path to reach your goal.

Here is an example of this:

Believing that all people on Earth are unique and valuable from birth, with a right to a healthy and happy life, is not a hard thing to do – it corresponds to widely accepted moral and human principles.

If you believe in this too, this being so positive and correct that I have no doubt that you do, then you should simply *apply the same principles to yourself.*

If you set out on this path, where you will fully accept and respect yourself as a valuable human being, then you will succeed in abandoning obsessive thinking about weight gain and weight loss as trivial and unimportant. You will be able to focus all your thoughts, with ease and pleasure, on something much more important and pleasant - health and happiness. Each day you will develop *consciously and in a focused manner*, an ever stronger wish to be healthy, strong, and happy in life, which is so positive and inspiring that no negative conviction will challenge it in your subconscious mind.

This will be the result of a new and comprehensive positive conviction you have adopted – consciously, with consideration and without resistance. Your new way of thinking will spontaneously "overwrite" all your previous, negative, subconscious convictions, just as a new song will be recorded over the previous one on a cassette tape.

This is how your *new positive attitudes about life*, supported by health and happiness, encompassing all aspects of your life, including your physical weight, will become *dominant* – both in your conscious and in your unconscious mind.

This implies no conflict between your wishes and your convictions, as both are in harmony and are equally positive.

This is why your new convictions will easily attract emotions to their positive side.

And what happens then?

Your behavior will spontaneously change, wholly and in the most positive sense.

Motivation and enthusiasm for exercise and a healthy,

moderate diet will surface on its own, bringing you the results desired - slowly, without effort and strain. You will burn excess fat in your body and reshape your muscles, in addition to a number of other health benefits.

Dear Petra, at the end, I am sending you some beautiful thoughts:

Things will happen the way you (really) believe they will!

If you firmly believe in Goodness – you will see Goodness all around you!

We shape our future with our convictions!

Regards, Dr. Tanya Skoro"

It is exceptionally important that you understand and adopt everything said here. Once you have done that, we can continue, since it will be easy for you to continue receiving new messages and lessons.

Life energy

Our own life energy is just a small part of the overall life energy, just as a drop in an ocean constitutes a part of the entire ocean.

Since the overall life energy is indivisible and omnipotent, so are our small parts of life energy, identical to the overall life energy – being equally omnipotent and omniscient.

At the time of your birth things were perfectly aligned for your development, since life energy creates harmony and well-being for all. There is no need for you to interfere with its work by your feeble attempts of willpower, which can only spoil what was created perfectly from the start.

In other words, every person is a masterpiece of nature, each one being complete and perfect in their own unique way. It is in diversity that the wealth of human potential lies, and we all must fully respect our originality and individuality.

Once you understand this, a huge burden and responsibility for your own life will be taken off your chest, giving you a break from worrying, allowing you to find peace and start enjoying your naturally perfect life.

Life energy wove special wishes and desires into you, gently indicating its plans for you, the true meaning of your life, and your purpose in life.

These wishes have existed in you since the beginning and have been present throughout your lifetime. They are what make us different and determine our separate individualities.

We can all recognize that our wishes in life have always been present, special and fully subjective, and thus very different from the wishes of other people.

For instance, think about it and you will realize this – some of the activities listed below have surely been your special wishes in life, too – painting, singing, playing music, dancing, researching, teaching, discovering, helping, fixing, constructing, growing, deciding, decorating, etc.

Life energy has discreetly directed each of us towards our perfection, through specific wishes. This is the special life plan.

This is why we should be deeply grateful and truly respect our lives. We show respect by living according to our inborn wishes and preferences, fulfilling our purpose in life through them as intended and to our own best benefit.

Trusting life energy

Life energy determined all our wishes and preferences at the time of birth. It also devised ways in which these wishes would come true. Rest assured, along with your wishes, you were also blessed with all the talents and abilities necessary to fulfill your wishes.

You were granted wishes precisely because life energy wants and expects their fulfillment in your lifetime.

I truly believe that each one of us received everything we need to live the life we want from life energy, as such a life was predetermined for us.

I also have no doubt that precisely such a spontaneous life is the best and happiest for everyone.

The simple conclusion here is that any violent and unnatural intentional intervention on your part can easily jeopardize your luck and the fate you desire.

And this is precisely what bulimic women do to themselves every day.

Once you have understood and accepted this, your new knowledge will result in full *comprehension of your own meaning in life*.

Open your mind to new discoveries, then just sit back and watch your life change for the better.

Along with these new convictions, your thoughts will spontaneously become positive, with full faith in well-being.

Let go and have full faith in the natural course of your life! Let your life energy flow, and it will immediately change your life, the way that works best for you.

Take a breath of relief, relax, let all of your worries and frantic efforts go, so that you can begin a calm life that is in harmony with itself and its own nature.

When you stop struggling to get something, knowing that you already possess everything you need, there will be absolutely no need for you to torture your body. On the contrary, everything that has not happened on its own, that you have tried to obtain by force and struggle, immediately reveals your distrust of life energy.

By doubting that you will get what you want, you are essentially sending a message to your life energy that you do not believe in its omnipotence, in the wishes it granted you, or in the existence of a perfect plan for you. This also means you believe that you are alone and abandoned, due to which you must take care of yourself and your lifestyle with your own willpower and effort. If you truly convince yourself of this, your willpower, combined with fear, will immediately step into your life. Together, they will initiate a bitter and useless battle with life, considering it to be the enemy.

In other words, the more you want to achieve something by force and with effort, doubting that this will happen spontaneously, the less success you will have!

The fierceness of your struggle and suffering indicates your own lack of faith that you will get what you want. The belief that life energy fulfills your wishes would be expressed by no struggle at all, but rather by patience as you wait for its realization.

Things will always be this way.

Whenever you believe that you do not have something you desperately want, what will come true is a reflection of your convictions, the opposite of your wishes, because you believe in the *non-existence* of your wishes, rather than in their *existence*.

When you believe in Evil, in a lack of Goodness, and that your life will have bad outcomes – then that is what your life will be like.

On the other hand, if you believe in the omnipotence and good intentions of life energy, then you will believe exclusively in Goodness, which will then be reciprocated back to you as well. This happens because the character of life energy is perfect harmony, unconditional love, and universal well-being.

You realize now that *everything that happens in your life depends on your trust in life energy.*

A person who trusts her life energy completely, who lives a peaceful, active, and loving life, in harmony with what has been predetermined for her, will see the fulfillment of her wishes without effort, like receiving a gift.

A person who does not believe in the well-being granted by life energy will spend her life fighting for the fulfillment of her wishes, believing that she must secure them on her own, certain she must fight alone for everything in life. The more one believes in this, the more evil and more failures will come their way, having attracted unwanted events in their life with fearful and untrusting thoughts.

So all of us will live precisely the life we believe in, deep inside.

Causes of physical problems

Your physical problems always stem from your system of convictions. You will only be able to restore your health if you succeed in changing your incorrect (negative) pattern of thought.

The desire and decision to change your patterns of thinking and feeling will surface only when you "wake up" and become aware of your immensely negative convictions and their consequences.

You will succeed in transforming your negative emotions into positive ones only when you truly believe in the omnipotence and good intentions of life energy. This belief will spontaneously *change all your attitudes about life into positive ones*. This is the only route for allowing your future to flow freely, spontaneously, and in a positive manner.

Every desire for success or cure will be efficient only when full faith in life or in the omnipotence of life energy has taken root in your soul. This trust must be absolute, without a shred of doubt, because only then will it eliminate all fear and failure from your life.

What we absolutely believe in becomes our truth in life and comes true!

All differences in our lives lie precisely in the convictions we carry in our hearts about ourselves and our lives.

A person living with thoughts of well-being will find well-being all around her.

If you develop a strong faith in Goodness in your heart, this will indicate your faith in life energy as well, and in a life you were destined to live. You will not want to correct and change it, attempting to transform it into what it is not – which is precisely what bulimics do, where they invest most of their efforts and err the most.

From now on you should perceive your life with unaltered faith as good and must deeply feel you are destined for happiness and love, not for suffering and struggle.

Forgive yourself for having strayed once - with a false conviction that you are betrayed and unloved.

That is when you stopped believing in the perfection of life energy. In your unreasonable fear of the future, you relied solely on yourself, although aware of how weak and helpless you are.

In your childish panic, you created a protective mental armor, hiding and locking yourself in it, along with your fear. As if you had made a subconscious sort of arrangement with yourself, promising yourself no one would ever hurt you again. You have decided to persevere in the siege imposed by life, convinced it brings nothing but suffering and pain. You were fully unaware that with this, you have prevented good things from entering your life.

By defending yourself from suffering, you destroyed happiness, renouncing the very possibility of love. And so your defense against pain became complete and efficient, but the price paid for it was too high.

The price for not feeling any suffering or pain was an empty life. It created a black hole in your soul, without any pain, but with no happiness either. No pain and no love.

Then you went a step further, believing in the assumed control, proud of the imaginary superiority that you had over your life. You wore your armor, not knowing the black hole would follow you everywhere.

Interesting, but no one, not even the people closest to you, noticed that they were living with a ghost, and that the authentic Ivana, Ana, or Maria had begun to disappear. They accepted you, loved you for what you were and took care of you. They may have noticed you were somewhat strange, exclusive, and whimsical, but they did not mind. You received plenty of love. The problem was that you could not receive it, as your armor was fully impenetrable. You had the feeling that nothing could break in.

What did you turn into after several years? On the outside you became beautiful but empty images; on the inside – scared victims. Years went by, it seems the defense contract had now expired, making your forget about the protective armor you still carried around.

It is a strange life you are living now.

You feel strange to yourself, both inside and out.

You are not like others.

You do not understand anything, except a lingering, constant sorrow. This sorrow will not let you love, and it forbids joy. It only brings a good understanding of someone else's sorrow. You always know what other miserable people feel in their souls, and which words will console them. To look into someone's sad eyes alone would be enough to learn their life story. You cannot understand why you only feel truly alive when you are helping other miserable people. You believe this may be because you were born with the talent of empathy. In fact, this is but a thin shred of love that has secretly escaped through a crack in your armor, swimming across the black lake in your soul. It managed to caress someone's face and brighten someone's day, with the right words and approach. This is why you enjoy real, sincere, and deep conversations with good people. Like radar, you discover miserable and unfortunate people in every group, and your soul runs to them. You extend your hands, because you can love only them. Perhaps this is because they too have their own armor and their black lake. Or maybe it is because they recognized you as well.

Perhaps miserable people feel better when they are together, as they are so similar inside and out. It is a familiar and comfortable atmosphere for them – they share the same cloud of despair.

It is different with happy people. You are clumsy around them. They somehow seem too lovely. The joy emanating from them is a continual surprise and seems to burn your cheeks. Perhaps it is because this feeling is unknown to you, and it seems unnecessary and superfluous.

The fact that they achieve everything with ease is astonishing. They have fun, eat and drink with ease, and succeed without effort. They do not get drunk or overweight and are not ugly. It is as if they had stars in their eyes. The world is equally crazy about them – returning their love, showering them with money, fame, success. . .

You do not like being envious, yet you wonder how they achieve it all. What is their secret that you are unable to learn? You would love to find out what it feels like to be happy and content. This desire is painful, making you feel like a spy in heaven.

You feel something is wrong with you, since you would otherwise be living a happy life as well. But you have not felt that way for a long time, nor have you had any other pleasant feelings, either. You know well the miserable ones and are close to them as if there was no other option. Feeling inseparable from them almost makes you feel as if you love them.

Your mind has always worked well, but why did it fail to realize where all this despair was coming from? It realized that something was wrong with your feelings – as if your sorrow would not let any happiness in. This is why you are unable to be happy when you wish, or calm when need to be. The closest feeling to this is when you are alone, stuffing yourself with chocolate, ice cream, and cake.

Moreover, it seems like these are the only moments when you love yourself. Like a mother feeding her infant, you feed your body a meal of satisfaction and peace. And then – horror and fear! You must prevent weight gain immediately and the food must come out.

And so "drugging" yourself with food became your only path to a "private heaven", the amount of the "drug" being your only measure of pleasure.

If you truly want to change everything and learn to live in a health, with love and joy, you must first learn to open the door of your prison-castle and find the way out, into real life.
Come with me, follow me out. Open your mind and heart wide. Nothing bad can happen to you on the path of truth.

The significance of mental attitude

Your way of thinking and believing, which creates a mental attitude, plays a decisive role in how you feel, your appearance, and how healthy you are.

What you perceive about yourself and your body every day turns into feelings about your body that ultimately materialize in reality. What is wrong is that most often you are thinking about the lack, rather than presence, of what you want. Perhaps you have already noticed that your thoughts revolve more around your failures than around advantages to your health, the lack of success rather than its existence, more around hardship than gain. Soon, this turns into strong patterns determining your lifestyle, thus becoming your truth in life, although your wishes are precisely the opposite.

A person will be in good health only with good thoughts, positive attitudes, and control over psychological enemies such as hatred, fear, and all negative emotions. You can assume psychological responsibility for your health by having healthy thoughts constantly circling, vibrating, and pulsing in your body.

Think well and you will feel well.

Attempt to maintain your peace and optimism at all times and under all circumstances, because every long-term perception of oneself ultimately becomes reality.

Fear of your future makes you obsess about problems and mishaps, filled with worry and fear that something disagreeable might happen.

It makes you observe others, envying those who have more, who are younger, more beautiful, and more successful than you. Your mind is constantly flooded with negative thoughts like dissatisfaction, fear, despair, bitterness, jealousy, fury, anger, and pity. Instead of thinking about what you have and what is good about your life, you are overwhelmed with thoughts of defeat and failure. These thoughts evoke negative feelings, making you disappointed with yourself, disheartened and depressed. This means that disease will disappear only when we lack faith in our health, obsessing and worrying only about the possibility of getting sick. If we are sick and do not believe in the power of our body and the intelligence of our cells, when we lack faith in the cure, disease will fully set in or even worsen.

This is why the transformation of negative and destructive emotions into positive moods filled with love always results in health and well-being.

Therefore, always think about your health, never about disease.

My dear readers, I hope it is now completely clear to you that by allowing bulimia to enter your lives, you have truly shown how much you distrust your life energy.

The basic spiritual law says that you will experience the things in your life that you constantly think about. They will surely appear, precisely in the form and with the significance you gave them in your thoughts and feelings.

It is interesting to analyze the manner in which a typical bulimic thinks. The essence is in understanding how she feels then, and comprehending which reality will be created in her life as a result of such thoughts and emotions.

This is the approximate train of thought a bulimic has from the moment she wakes up in the morning:

How awful, I am awake again.

I am expected to live again.
To get up, organize my day, and eat a healthy diet.
To study and prepare for the exam.
To have plenty of energy and be cheerful.
To call my folks and give them an update.
To tell them everything is fine with me and how my life is wonderful.
Just what they expect.
To go out and buy healthy food then. To not be tempted to buy food to stuff myself with.
To be calm, happy, cheerful, and content...
And naturally, my boyfriend expects a cute, smiling girlfriend.
Always in the mood for cuddling and sex.
Always guessing and fulfilling all his expectations.
Yeah right!

What is wrong with them all? Everyone is expecting something from me, and I am a thousand light years away. They have no idea how bad the despair and pain that I wake up and go to bed with are. They are clueless about how much I hate this life of mine and my incompetence in it.

Oh, I have to get up now and weigh myself. This is terrible, as if I were going to be executed. Either way, regardless of how I feel, I have to know whether to mark this day with a plus or a minus.

I am sure that if the scale shows a higher number, I will seriously want to kill myself. If I see a number higher than the one I am aiming for, I will want to disappear. I will want to remove myself from this world which knows nothing but insults, demands, and judgment.

Well, my dear, here you are making plans when you do

not even have the energy to get up, let alone kill yourself.
Fine, I get it, I won't kill myself today, but what I can do instead is go on a magnificent eating binge. I am killing myself with that too, but slowly and gradually.
What if the scale shows less than yesterday?
Then I will get a rare shot of energy – as a reward, to celebrate.
But what is my biggest prize, my ultimate pleasure? Naturally, a magnificent binge to sweeten my morning and the new day. Then I will go on several smaller binges, just to become numb, to not think, to wrap up and hide my new fear of the number on the scale tomorrow, my fear of yet another day.
So there you are, my loser, whatever you do, you end up with a binge. It is the only winner and the only certainty in your daily life.
And since I feel so weak after every binge and vomiting that I am dizzy, studying is out of the question and impossible. In this condition, how will I be able to concentrate on anything except my distress and self-hatred, my growing feeling of failure, my desire to give up on everything, especially living with myself.
You are so disgusting. How long are you planning to go on like this? You are going to ruin yourself entirely! Why can't you be normal like other girls, like the rest of the world? Why don't you have any energy; why are you just lazing around? Why can't you wash up and get dressed? All you do is mope around, nervous, hating yourself and doing nothing but crying, crying, crying . . .?
Will anyone help me? But I don't want to see anyone!
Will you end up all shriveled up in your own puke?
O God, this is too hard. Help me, please help me, I can't do this alone.

These thoughts and feelings echo in the minds of bulimics every morning, wherever they are in the world. They are all desperate in their fear of the disease holding them in its steel grip.

Let us analyze these thoughts.

They are all extremely negative, accompanied by equally negative emotions: pity, sorrow, pain, self-hatred, suffering, depression.

The depression never goes away.

What kind of energy can such a person emit?

She can only send negative vibrations! She can only emit the energy of despair and suffering.

Unhappy thoughts will attract other unhappy thoughts, lasting for days, months, and years...

Finally, this negative energy will become a set framework determining her life.

Although bulimics occasionally find the strength to think about a solution to their problems, they still constantly dwell upon their problems.

Thus, problems remain present in their lives at all times.

This is what bulimia feeds upon.

No medication can reverse this pattern.

How is it possible then, if it is possible at all, for them to escape from the bulimic circle of hell?

It is possible, but only by changing the pattern of thought that created the problem in the first place!

Her mental attitude about herself and her life must transform from negative to positive.

Hatred and fear must be replaced by a deep and complete acceptance of herself and her life, despite the problems that exist.

Here is what this means in practice.

Every bulimic is obsessively focused on nothing but her own problems and constantly thinks about them. She is completely wrapped up in her negative thoughts, reinforced by identical, extremely negative and unpleasant feelings.

If she is ready to change that and get better, a bulimic must undergo a spiritual and mental transformation, and she must be determined in her decision change course. Faith in life energy will help her realize this transformation.

This is the turning point where she must stop obsessing about everything *she does not want*, and begin thinking about *what she does want* in her life.

Think about health, not disease. About success, not defeat. About giving, not taking.

In other words, the most important step is to activate your thoughts and keep them focused on the changes you desire. The rest will happen spontaneously, without strain or effort.

You may already have heard or read somewhere that a person controls her life by controlling her thoughts. Perhaps it was not clear to you, being unaware of the spiritual law where identical vibrations are mutually attracted. I hope that you can understand and accept this fact now.

It is simple to find out whether you are successful in your attempts to think positive thoughts. Just ask yourself how you feel and try to identify your emotions precisely. Name them.

Feelings are your most valuable ally in the process of change, unequivocally indicating whether your thoughts are positive or whether you have reverted back to your previous, negative patterns.

When your previous, negative emotions creep back in, you will recognize them immediately by feeling anxious. In that case, the most important thing to keep reminding yourself is: *"My life energy will show me the way to happiness. I trust it and believe in it. Everything will be all right."*

Slowly and gently plan to do something good for yourself.

Trust your new, positive thoughts and you will succeed!

Be patient with yourself. Rest assured that your life energy will lead and direct you to your desired goal.

Every day, try to think in a positive manner, and repeat slowly: I was born perfect and blessed.

Every person on this planet deserves to love and be loved, and so do I.

It is wonderful that we are all unique and different; this is truly what makes life valuable.

Since every person, unique in their imperfection, is still worthy of love, then I too am worthy of love. Just like this, imperfect, like the others. I do not have to wait endlessly to become perfect first in order to start accepting and loving myself and others. It is perfectly normal to love myself now, regardless of my weight, years, intelligence or looks.

I do not have to suffer any longer!

I am allowed to be unconditionally happy. I was given this permission and obligation from my life energy, just like every other person in the world.

We are all one, as parts of the same life energy. This is why I love myself by loving others, and by loving myself, I love others.

Life is good and filled with joy.

Everything is fine and will continue to remain fine."

By repeating these statements and believing in them, you eliminate mental blocks, gradually transforming negative emotions into positive ones.

That is the real way out.

If you make a conscious effort to retain your new, positive thoughts in your mind longer and allow them to stabilize, an overall feeling of well-being and contentment will take over for good.

Basic human needs

Human beings resemble one another in a number of ways. Their basic needs in life, physical, psychological and spiritual, are almost identical.

A person can achieve harmony in her life, accompanied with a feeling of contentment and happiness, only if her basic human needs have been fulfilled. In a way, their fulfillment is a precondition for a general feeling of happiness and well-being. We have to fulfill our human needs every day, and each day is a miniature life of its own. It must become a habit like brushing our teeth – we don't think about it, but we do it anyway.

Human beings have six basic human needs – one physiological, four psychological, and one spiritual need. They cannot be happy until these needs have been fulfilled. Even when only one is missing, it brings down the entire structure of happiness. This rule applies to bulimics as well, the difference being that almost none of their basic needs are fulfilled. This is precisely why all bulimics, without exception, constantly feel unhappy and incomplete.

These needs surface in a specific order, since every subsequent need is expressed only after previous ones have been fulfilled. I will list them below in their natural sequence.

1. Physical survival – this is a physiological need determined by the structure of the genes in our body, expressed by the *minimum conditions* necessary for a person's physiological existence. It includes the need for air, water, food, shelter and the continuation of the species (reproduction).

When all the necessary needs are fulfilled for physical

existence, four basic psychological needs surface, related to survival, as they make survival more successful and pleasant. In the presentation of these needs, I will use the well-known classification of psychological needs described by Dr. William Glasser.

The basic psychological needs are:

2. *Love and belonging* - when physical existence needs have been fulfilled, a person as a social being develops a psychological need to belong to another person or group (family, relatives, friends, clubs, and the like), with whom they can develop a relationship of closeness, acceptance, and love.

3. *Power and recognition* - when the two previous needs have been fulfilled, a strong need for self-confidence and self-respect develops, as well as acceptance and respect by one's environment. Humans are the only species driven by a desire for power. The need to have power influences the life we choose. We want to be winners and control things and other people alike. It also encompasses the need for material symbols of power: to obtain titles, functions, money, and objects like houses, cars, expensive clothes, and the like.
Once the first three needs have been fulfilled, a new one emerges – freedom.

4. *Freedom* in essence indicates a human need to *have choices*. We are free only when we are able to decide on our own, without being forced, about where, how, and with whom we want to live, what we want to do, and which moral, political, and spiritual principles we want to follow.
Once a person has fulfilled her need for existence, love, power and freedom, the need to have fun and enjoy life appears.

5. Fun - enjoying life – this encompasses socializing with friends, hobbies, and everything we love and enjoy doing. Unfortunately, it also encompasses addiction, as a negative example of enjoyment with negative consequences (smoking, alcoholism, drug consumption, overeating, gambling, etc.).

These needs, typical for all of us, are complemented by one more, which I consider to be the final basic human need, which harmoniously joins and raises awareness about all human efforts, and which is essential for giving meaning to life. *This is the need for spiritual fulfillment.* Although not all people will develop this need, a majority will. It is particularly characteristic of persons with a high level of consciousness.

6. Spiritual fulfillment is manifested in the feeling of physical and spiritual existence united into one, expressed through the consciousness of one's purpose in life.

Since only a person who has fulfilled all her basic human needs can live a happy and meaningful life, we can analyze our lives every day, as well as those of others, if we know the circumstances they live in. This analysis will allow us to easily evaluate to what extent we have fulfilled these important needs for ourselves, providing us also with the answer to how happy we or others are.

Let us see how bulimics fulfill these basic human needs:

1. The first human need – survival is almost always fulfilled in bulimics. Most of them being young, they usually live with their parents, who take care of them.
2. The second basic human need, exceptionally important – *love and belonging*, remains unfulfilled in bulimics. Deep

down they are aware that their parents love them, but they suffer immensely when they see that parental love is not unconditional, that it is in fact very conditional. Moreover, suffering because they are not loved unconditionally, which they desperately want, bulimics become fully incapable of loving anyone else, because the precondition for this is that bulimics love and accept themselves first, which is the main problem and obstacle in bulimia. Thus bulimics have a problem both with loving and being loved, which has a decisive influence on all their needs in life. Being depressed, they are always somewhat isolated from others, constantly feeling lonely and misunderstood. The need for belonging, both to a family and to any other group, is therefore never fulfilled. This is why bulimics face a closed door leading to happiness, already at their second need in life.

3. *Power* as a need always remains unfulfilled in bulimics, who are insecure and have an inferiority complex. They lack self-confidence and self-respect, and are thus unable to give it to others, except when feigning it. Others feel this and, as a result, never show them the respect, consideration, and admiration that they desire so much.

4. *Freedom,* or the possibility of choice, is something bulimics do not have, and they suffer for it. They are forced by their addiction to go on eating binges, which strips them of the will, desire, and energy to do anything else in life.

5. *Fun and the enjoyment of life* in bulimics is almost always fulfilled with their addiction to food, with binge eating that psychologically replaces healthy entertainment, as well as being loved and loving others.

6. Bulimics are *spiritually empty*, although they are looking for answers about their purpose and meaning in life.

You understand now why you must be miserable if you have bulimia, but I do hope you have realized by now that happiness does not have to remain out of your reach.
Leading a happy life is actually very simple – one only needs to learn how to best fulfill her basic human needs.
Each one of us must fulfill our needs in our own specific way, and as long as this implies healthy and positive means, you too will have full freedom in this.

The best and quickest way to learn to live a happy life is by structuring your day and writing notes in your *Behavior and Daily Analysis Journal*.

A structured day

Every morning you should plan how your day will be structured and enter it into your journal. These should be predetermined activities listed in chronological order. You must plan them by bearing in mind how to best fulfill all six of your basic needs.

I will walk you through it based on Marta's example.
Having joined the Overcoming Bulimia Program, Marta was close to being cured.
Bent over her journal one morning with pen in hand, Marta wrote down the following thoughts:

> My parents sent me money yesterday – I can pay for the dorm for next month, buy food and the books I need, and I'll still have some pocket money left. This fulfills my first basic need, *survival,* today.

I will call my mom to thank her, and will talk to my dad and sister as well. I will give them a hug in my mind, and will not forget to tell them how much I love them. I know they love me back and that we belong together, which means that I will fulfill my second basic need today – the need for *love and belonging*.

Last night I studied hard for today's test, I am confident I have studied everything, I am calm and expect a good grade. This means that I have self-confidence and that I respect myself. My professor will respect me too, which will give me a wonderful feeling of *power and recognition*, fulfilling my third basic need.

My fourth need, *freedom*, is fulfilled by the fact that I am studying what I am interested in, that I live in a dorm I like, and because I spend my days the way I choose. My freedom of choice is everything that matters in my life now.

After my test I will go to the dining hall for a healthy lunch. Then I will relax for two hours, and go to a salsa course with my roommate. We will enjoy the music and dance together. Perhaps that new guy, Ivan, will decide to dance with me . . . This is sufficient to fulfill my fifth basic need – *fun*.

I have spent 20 minutes in bed this morning meditating and visualizing my goals. I felt complete and calm, sure of myself in going where my life energy takes me. This fulfills my sixth basic need – *spiritual fulfillment* – so I will feel satisfied and happy at the end of the day.

Tomorrow I will plan another happy day for myself.

I am now sure, as long as I live this way, my cravings for binge eating will not resurface, since they have become unnecessary and needless. They are only a memory from the past, where they were an attempt to replace all my basic needs that were unfulfilled in the most negative way of all.

I am happy knowing that by taking care of and loving myself, I spontaneously fulfill my basic needs, which keeps bulimia locked in my distant past, as a previous experience and a warning."

Your pattern of thought will resemble Marta's once you too embark on the Overcoming Bulimia Program. You may also be able to advise your friends as well, being aware of how well they are fulfilling their basic needs, since you know exactly what they may be missing in life and how that can be fixed.

Behavior and Daily Analysis Journal

You will have to write in your behavior journal every day, it being your most important companion on the road to change. The journal has specific sections to be completed every day, in order to clearly visualize everything that happens to you in the course of a day.

The journal encompasses all important areas of your life: diet, activities, relationships, work, fun, emotions, plans, and goals. It enables you to plan your day in the morning, listing the activities that fulfill your basic needs, whereas in the evening you can enter a summary of your day and analyze it. This will give you a clear idea of what you have experienced each day, how close you are to your goal, and how successful you are at reaching it.

I created the behavior and emotions journal in such a way that it becomes a safe guide through the Overcoming Bulimia Program, and as long as you observe its rules, your life will be healthy, balanced, and happy, a long way from depression and bulimia.

You will notice that the journal has several fixed boxes that must be completed daily, along with realistic self-analysis and correction "in stride".

BEHAVIOR JOURNAL

DIET (Food I have eaten)	
Breakfast – time:	
Lunch – time:	
Dinner – time:	
Eating binges:	No or yes (describe them)

ACTIVITIES	
Rest, university, going out, etc. (duration):	
Practice (sport and duration):	

DAILY ANALYSIS (answer the following questions in a few sentences)	
How do I feel?	
What am I thinking about?	
Which problems are bothering me?	

Decisions	
What was bad today?	
What was good today?	

You should note only what you actually ate for each meal in the *Diet* section (not the things you should be eating). At the end of the day, this will allow you to assess whether you followed the Diet Program.

The *Activities* section should contain your activities in the course of a day, so that you can assess whether they are taking you in a desired – positive – direction (like attending classes at university, resting, going to a coffee shop, socializing with friends).

The *Athletics* section should contain information about whether you exercised that day, which is advisable for maintaining good physical condition and a healthy weight.

You should complete the *eating binges* box by indicating whether you went on any eating binges that day or not. If you did have any binges, do not panic, just describe them in detail, along with the accompanying emotions. Then calmly, as if nothing happened, continue with your activities from the Program. Life according to the Program will have a healing effect, neutralizing and reversing the results of this "accident", allowing you to successfully return to the "health zone".

At the end of every day, you will be looking forward to facing the most important section - *Daily analysis*. In it, you will deal with your emotions. You are already aware of their critical significance, emotions being true masters of your overall behavior.

In this section you have to describe, in as much detail as possible, how you felt during the day, what you thought about, whether something bothered you or made you happy. You have to grade your daily emotions and describe them.

Then compare your emotions to your behavior during this day. Think about the thoughts you had that day, remind yourself of how positive and creative you have been. Moreover, make a note of any (remaining) negative convictions that may have spoiled a part of your day.

Analyze your thoughts, emotions, and behavior in detail. Try to discover your formula for success or failure. Always be aware that both are an integral part of life. Mistakes are a part of life. A positive transformation of your pattern of thought will always positively change your mood as well as the final outcome of every activity.

Daily journaling introduces the essential feature of critical objectivity into your life. It has decisive significance for your success in overcoming bulimia, as it does for your adjustment to a healthy and structured life.

Assuming the role of an objective observer of all events in the course of each day, you will be able to understand and assess the results of your decisions and behavior.

When you analyze in detail the complex picture recorded in your journal, it will be clear what your pattern of thought was like and what you were feeling that day. You will know exactly what kind of a person you have become, and what your life is like.

It is only when you fully understand and accept yourself that you gain the ability to change things you dislike into something new and better.

PART FIVE
PROPER AND HEALTHY DIET

Help the "child in you"

I hope I have been able to help you focus on positive thinking, so that, down the road, you will learn to accept yourself, which is the main precondition for curing bulimia.

From now on, try to treat yourself the way your best friend would treat you if you were in trouble. What would she do? She would invest all her efforts and imagination into helping and understanding you, and never – ever – would she criticize or blame you. Become your own best friend today – show understanding and love for yourself always, regardless of what happens to you in life.

Today, you are adults hoping to become healthy and happy, but you must not neglect an important part of you, which has been active all along – your "inner" child. This part of you is emotionally immature, and thus completely unstable in its reactions. It is precisely this inner child, the "little girl" in you, that suffers from bulimia. She is genuinely unhappy and extremely sad, but just underneath her seemingly passive sorrow, lie strong emotions of anxiety, rage, and fury.

Become a mother to this unhappy girl inside you today, and love her unconditionally, because this is what she needs the most. The easiest way to do this is by visualizing that you consist of two inseparable parts - one being the *inner child*, a sick, bulimic girl, and the other - *the adult that you are*. As of today, the *adult* has an obligation to help her *girl* heal, grow up, mature emotionally, and understand and balance out her life, in order to merge spontaneously with the adult you into a single, healthy, and happy being. To fulfill this imperative and

137

beautiful goal, you must start caring for your little girl already today. Take her through each day patiently – feed her healthy foods, entertain her until she laughs, give her creative activities to do, spend time with her, console and comfort her when she needs it, and above all – always show her your unconditional love, even at times when she is exhausting or aggressive.

By helping the girl within you heal, you slowly heal yourself. By loving her unconditionally, you actually love yourself.

In patiently coping with her despair, anxiety, and rage, you are in fact learning to accept yourself – for better or worse.

The final result will be a mature adult – a healed, healthy "child inside you". This will make your life wholesome, balanced, and happy.

As the *adult mother*, you will have to accomplish four significant things for the sick *girl inside you*.

- Teach her to accept herself and her life as a wholesome, unique gift of life, filled with love. This acceptance leads to unconditional love of oneself.
- Free her from her bulimic addiction to carbohydrates.
- Teach her to eat a healthy diet.
- Teach her about the proper structuring of time, so that her most important life needs can be fulfilled.

Let's get started!

About food

The key to bring a destabilized metabolic process back into balance is a healthy diet, according to the rules contained in the Overcoming Bulimia Program.

Food is what created your problem, and food is also your cure!

So let's talk about food.

The food we eat contains proteins, fats, carbohydrates, vitamins, minerals, and water, all of which break down in the body, with the final process being the growth and regeneration of damaged cells, the growth of different tissues, and the creation of energy necessary for all the activities of the mind and body.

All food that we eat is digested immediately. Once ingested, food undergoes a number of very complex chemical processes when breaking down and transforming (metabolism), then enters the bloodstream through the intestinal wall, and is distributed throughout the body to be used.

Fats

Fats are fatty substances from animal or plant sources. Once digested, they are absorbed in the blood in the form of fatty acids.

Fats are an essential part of any diet, having a crucial role in numerous metabolic functions (in the composition of cell membranes, tissues, nerve cells, and hormones, they are necessary for breaking down fat-soluble vitamins, and are a source of energy and more.)

Small amounts of fats are sufficient for our physical needs, while an excessive intake of fats and an inadequate selection may seriously endanger one's health.

According to their chemical structure, we distinguish between saturated and unsaturated fatty acids, which have different effects on our health.

Saturated fatty acids come from animal sources – fats from meat and meat products, eggs, and dairy products.

An excessive portion of these fats boosts the increase of triglycerides and bad cholesterol in the blood, causing cardiovascular diseases and weight gain.

The transformation of saturated fats into fat deposits in the body is linked to the combination of these fats with carbohydrates, and to the resulting presence of insulin in the blood.

Unsaturated fatty acids consist of monounsaturated, polyunsaturated and trans-unsaturated fatty acids.

Monounsaturated fatty acids are found in olive oil and are very healthy, especially for the cardiovascular system.

Polyunsaturated fatty acids are found in linseed, sunflower, corn, and peanut oil and in fish oils such as tuna, salmon, and pilchard (omega 3 fatty acids). These are beneficial fats with a good influence on our health.

Trans-unsaturated fatty acids come from plant sources, but their structure has been changed during industrial or culinary processing (margarines, lard for semi-cooked meals, and fat in overcooked meat). These have a detrimental influence on our health, contributing to cardiovascular disease.

Proteins

Proteins are the main building material of our bodies, being the main structural ingredient in all our cells. Amino acids, which proteins are composed of, are the basis of all forms of life.

There are twenty key amino acids. The body is unable to synthesize eight of them, known as essential amino acids, which is why we have to ingest them with food. If our body does not receive these amino acids regularly, the production of new proteins will slow down and in extreme cases will cease entirely.

Proteins from animal sources (meat, eggs, fish, dairy) are complete, containing all the essential amino acids (the ones our bodies cannot synthesize on their own), while proteins from *plant sources* (in grains, legumes, beans, and seeds) do not contain them and are thus incomplete, requiring combining (either with other plant sources or with proteins from animal sources).

Carbohydrates

How can we recognize carbohydrate foods?

It is all food containing *sugar* and *starch*. The most significant carbohydrate foods are:

- *all desserts* (chocolate, candy, cookies, cakes, ice-cream, creams, puddings and others, all of which contain sugar);
- *flour-based foods* (pasta, cream of wheat, bread, pastries, pizza, salty phyllo dough, pies, strudels and others, all of which contain starch);
- *rice* (containing large amounts of starch);
- *grains and grain products* (wheat, rye, oats, barley, and others, all containing starch);
- *legumes* (beans, peas, broad beans, soy, lentils, chick-peas and others, all containing starch);
- *vegetables*, primarily roots (potatoes, beets, turnips, carrots, and the like);
- *fruit* – mostly sweet and dried fruits.

All carbohydrates undergo the chemical processes of digestion in the body, and at the end of this process all, without exception, are transformed into blood sugar – *glucose*. The glucose created in this way enters the bloodstream through the intestinal wall, and its levels in the blood increase (*glycemia*). The *pancreas* reacts to the surge in glycemia. It is the most important organ in the metabolizing carbohydrates, and it is essential for the metabolism in general.

The pancreas responds to the surge of glucose in the blood by excreting the hormone insulin, the task of which is to bring glycemia back down to a normal level and to transport glucose to the liver (which then stores it for future use in the form of glycogen-) and to muscles, which turn it into energy and use it. When a huge amount of carbohydrates enters the body at one time, its digestion will create a significant amount of glucose, so insulin will be forced to use the surplus glucose in the process of lipogenesis, creating fat deposits in the body.

Of all the food types, only carbohydrates have the ability to cause a metabolic condition similar to nicotine, alcohol, and drug addiction. This is why it is precisely carbohydrates that have a crucial role in the onset and long-term duration of bulimia. They are the culprit in bulimic binge eating, and only planned control of their intake can solve this problem.

Proteins and fats, on the other hand, will never lead to addiction, regardless of the amounts or frequency of their intake, since their metabolizing does not lead to the excretion of the hormone insulin, which is crucial in the onset of addiction.

Glycemic index

Not all carbohydrates have the same metabolic values. They differ in the amount of glucose created in the blood - their *glycemic potential.*

For instance, the digestion of a cake containing lots of sugar (sucrose) will result in a larger amount of glucose absorbed in the blood from the intestines, causing a high glycemic response, while the digestion of rye bread will release much less glucose, and the glycemic response will accordingly be lower. This difference is a result of their molecular structure, which determines the speed at which they break down in the intestines. This means that each carbohydrate is specific.

The amount of glucose in the blood produced in the process of digesting a carbohydrate, which is a specific glycemic response (the level of glycemia reached) to the intake of a specific carbohydrate, is referred to by scientists as the carbohydrate's *glycemic index (GI).*

A glycemic index determines the degree to which a certain carbohydrate increases the level of glucose in the blood.

Scientists have established sugar as the basis for comparison, having allocated it an index of 100. According to a specific formula and the values of resulting glycemia, they have calculated an index for all other carbohydrates.

This is how the *glycemic index table* was created.

This table serves as a practical and useful indicator of the influence each carbohydrate has on the body, and helps determine their health benefits or detrimental effects.

According to glycemic index values, scientists have divided all carbohydrates into two groups –*good* ones and *bad* ones.

Glycemic index table

"BAD" carbohydrates	GI
White flour	125
Maltose (beer)	110
White crystal sugar (sucrose)	100
Corn	95
Potato	95
Honey	90
White rice	85
Cooked carrots	85
Dried fruit	70
Bananas	70
White flour pasta (cooked *al'dente*)	60

"GOOD" carbohydrates	GI
Wholegrain (unprocessed) grains (wheat, rye, oats, barley, bran)	50
Wholegrain (brown) rice	50
Peas, beans, and other legumes	50
Oat bran	40
Wholegrain pasta (brown, cooked *al'dente*)	40
Rye bread	40
Dairy products	35
Fruit ice creams with artificial sweeteners	35
Fresh fruit (except bananas)	30
Fruit marmalade with no sugar	30
Dark chocolate (>70% cocoa)	25
Fructose (fruit sugar)	20

Soy and all soy products	20
Peanuts, seeds, nuts	15
Green vegetables, button mushrooms	10
Tomatoes	10
Lemon and grapefruit	10

"Bad" carbohydrates are those with a GI higher than 50, meaning that a large amount of glucose is released when digested, resulting in glycemia much higher than normal. This causes a release of a sudden, large amount of insulin from the pancreas. A high level of insulin in the blood will turn excess glucose into fat deposits, causing weight gain.

Carbohydrates have the highest glycemic index and are the major part of junk food – popular food in rich, industrial countries, which has caused the current obesity epidemic. It primarily consists of refined (processed) products like sugar, white flour, and white rice.

In industrial processing, the initial whole, unprocessed ingredients (sugar cane, sugar beet, wheat, and brown rice) are stripped of practically all nutrients (fibers, vitamins and minerals), resulting in tasty products (white bread and pastry, cakes, creams, chocolate, and others) which are easily and quickly digested, but apart from calories, have no nutritional value.

Precisely due to their easy and fast digestion, carbohydrates with a high GI cause an exceptional rise in the blood sugar level, resulting in a significant excretion of the "fattening" hormone, insulin, into the bloodstream.

As a result, carbohydrates with high GIs are also referred to as "hyperglycemic" food.

Regular intake of large amounts of carbohydrates with high glycemic indices (fast food diets, typical in the US), initiates metabolic reactions in the body, leading to hyperinsulinemia (creating fat deposits), which is the main cause of obesity.

"Good" carbohydrates are those with GIs lower than 50, meaning that a comparably small amount of glucose is released by digestion. For this reason, glycemia does not rise significantly, causing a small (or insignificant) excretion of insulin, which is beneficial for the body, since fat deposits and weight gain will not occur.

Good carbohydrates include all *whole* (unprocessed, unrefined) *grains, legumes, fruits* (those containing fruit sugar or fructose with exceptionally low GIs – 20) and *green, leafy vegetables.* These carbohydrates are exceptionally rich in *fiber*, the main characteristic of which is that it slows down and lowers the absorption of glucose from the intestines into the blood. This is the mechanism that lowers the glycemic potential of unprocessed foods.

The glycemic index will be very important in the next chapter, where I will discuss putting together healthy meals, and will use it as an example of how bulimic "addiction" to carbohydrates develops.

Insulin and serotonin

Two substances in the body – the hormone *insulin*, excreted by the pancreas, and the neurotransmitter *serotonin* in the brain – play the main role in the onset and duration of addiction to carbohydrates. Their interdependence is significant when metabolizing food, and in the regulation of hunger and fullness. While insulin "produces" the craving for carbohydrates, serotonin is able to reduce this craving, and even eliminate it.

Insulin is a hormone produced in the pancreas.
The pancreas excretes insulin into the bloodstream, but this only occurs when the blood sugar level (glycemia) exceeds the normal range. The task of the excreted insulin is to lower the increased level of glucose in the blood back to its normal

range.

Blood glucose levels will increase only when carbohydrates are ingested. I hope you remember that all carbohydrates, regardless of whether they are sweet or salty, turn to glucose when digested.

Unlike carbohydrates, proteins and fats will never turn to glucose when ingested, and will neither raise glucose levels in the blood, nor stimulate the excretion of insulin by the pancreas.

In other words, of all the foods available, insulin excretion from the pancreas into the bloodstream is linked only and exclusively to the consumption of carbohydrates.

Insulin is the most important hormone in metabolizing carbohydrates, as it maintains normal glucose levels in the blood. Once carbohydrates are ingested, a significant amount of glucose is produced in the blood, and glycemia rises. The pancreas will react to this immediately, excreting insulin into the bloodstream, with the aim of lowering the high glycemia back to a normal range.

Once this happens, insulin sends the excess glucose to the liver (depositing reserves in the form of glycogen) and the muscles, where this glucose is used as fuel for physical activity, while excessive amounts are turned to fat and stored in fat cells in the form of fat deposits.

In healthy persons, the amount of insulin excreted always corresponds exactly to the level of glycemia increase. For instance, when very high amounts of carbohydrates are ingested (bulimic binge eating), a large amount of glucose is created with the digestion of the food, and its levels in the blood will become extremely high. The pancreas then reacts accordingly, releasing a high amount of insulin into the blood. The insulin excreted lowers glucose levels with such force that its level in the blood drops below the normal range, creating the condition of "functional" hypoglycemia.

Since sugar levels in the blood below a normal range are exceptionally dangerous (potentially causing hypoglycemic coma), raising and balancing out hypoglycemia becomes the first priority of the brain. This evokes an uncontrollable craving for more sweet food. The brain must ensure a new intake of carbohydrates at whatever the cost, creating a feeling of hunger stronger than willpower. This is why the brain "forces" a person to eat carbohydrates again, regardless of her wishes. This produces new glucose, fulfilling its task, as it quickly raises sugar levels in the blood back to normal.

When a person eats a small amount of carbohydrates, her blood sugar level will get back to normal. However, in bulimics this amount is never small. Their new craving for sweet food will be exceptionally strong, since the previous meal consisted of a *binge*, not of a moderate increase in the amount of ingested carbohydrates. This is why functional hypoglycemia is always severe in bulimics, where the only compensation is a new bulimic eating binge, again with excessive amounts of "bad" carbohydrates. Glycemia will again significantly exceed normal limits, and the whole previous process will be repeated – the pancreas will release a large amount of insulin, which will then lower the blood sugar level below the normal range again, and a new craving for sweet food will occur.

This is the mechanism that maintains a constant craving for carbohydrates in bulimics, repeatedly generating new eating binges.

In the initial stage of bulimia, this craving is relatively mild, and the amounts of ingested carbohydrates are accordingly low, but over time it develops into a real, irresistible craving for carbohydrates, with all the typical characteristics of an addiction. Binge eating with "bad" carbohydrates then become more frequent, the amounts of the food necessary becoming ever larger.

You surely understand now that the bulimic craving for carbohydrates is not a psychological craving, but a physiological one – demanded by the body and resulting from a metabolic disorder. This is why it is always stronger than willpower, and bulimics have no choice but to fulfill it by constantly repeating their eating binges.

Once this vicious bulimic circle is metabolically created and sealed, it is endless.

Understanding this metabolic process is very important in order for you to realize that you have not consciously and through some fault of your own, created your "addiction" to carbohydrates, but that you have accidentally caused a metabolic disorder in your body, which is now keeping you pegged in the "addiction".

This is also important for parents to realize, as most of them believe that their daughter is deliberately and consciously choosing to remain sick, convinced that she could stop her binge eating with her willpower.

Several desperate fathers have asked me the following: "Tell me, please, what kind of force should I use? Should I spank her to make her stop overeating and vomiting?"

Once I have explained the metabolic causes of overeating, these fathers are usually in tears, angry at themselves for not knowing this, and for having suggested that physically hurting their beloved child might have helped.

I then remind them that they too, during the Christmas and New Year's holidays, have trouble resisting cake and cookies. Once they understood the process, all parents without exception have shown sympathy for their sick child, ready to support her with their love and care, instead of fighting and threatening them.

I want to stress that practically anyone could develop this "addiction" to carbohydrates if her diet consisted regularly of large amounts of pastry products, chocolate, cake, pizza, and other fast foods. Moreover, all obese persons have already developed this "addiction" to a certain extent, which is why hyperinsulinemia has created fat deposits in their bodies.

For bulimics, the insulin effect is not limited to the metabolic activity described above. Insulin, as the most potent hormone in food digestion, influences all other hormones and enzymes as well.

A raised level of insulin in the blood has three different effects on weight gain, due to which it has acquired the nicknames "hunger hormone" and "main fattening hormone" in the medical field.

The three fattening effects of raised insulin levels in the blood are the following:

1. *It causes the feeling of constant hunger*, but not for all food, only for carbohydrates (hunger hormone);

2. *It stimulates the transformation of ingested food to fat;*

3. *It prevents the burning* of existing fat deposits in the body (lipogenesis).

The first effect is created through the mechanism of functional hypoglycemia that I described earlier.

The second effect results from the fact that insulin is in charge during the process of digestion – as long as there is insulin in blood, it directs the biochemical processes of creating fat and storing it in the form of fat deposits in the body. The chemical processes of transforming food into fat are impossible without insulin.

This is why food containing fat but not carbohydrates (meat, fatty fish, eggs, fatty cheese) cannot create fat in the body (without carbohydrates). The reason for this is that fat is never transformed into glucose in the process of digestion, which leaves glucose levels in the blood intact, and therefore, the pancreas does not release insulin.

The third effect is that, as long as there is insulin in the blood, the chemical break-down of fats produced earlier is not possible.

Conclusion - when there is an excessive intake of carbohydrates, the insulin always, through its three "fattening" effects, successfully leads down a one-way street to weight gain. Fats are quickly created in the body, but are digested slowly, which co-occurs with the inability to stop eating carbohydrates.

To make matters more dangerous, carbohydrates (sugar and flour) always show up together with fats in precisely those foods (chocolate, ice-cream, cake, cookies, and pastry) which bulimics crave the most and always consume during their binge eating.

A combination of carbohydrates and fats leads to the fastest weight gain, since carbohydrates cause hyperinsulinemia, while insulin uses fatty acids as the perfect material for the production of fat deposits in the system.

The result of the overall effect of increased insulin in blood ultimately comes down to the production of fat deposits in the body, which justifies its nickname - "the main fattening hormone".

Your next question is surely why bulimics are not overweight, even though they consume large amounts of carbohydrates, forcing the pancreas to frequently release large amounts of insulin into the blood.

Bulimics eat a lot of carbohydrates and significant amounts of fat. This creates a large amount of glucose, and the pancreas releases high amounts of insulin into the blood, all of which should cause significant weight gain. Despite this, bulimics are always thin, oftentimes even underweight!

Are they a metabolic exception, being able to eat huge amounts of sweet and fatty foods without gaining weight?

No, bulimics are no exception, they are only inventive!

After every eating binge, they immediately induce vomiting, thereby discharging the food eaten from their system before insulin can turn it into fat. Some bulimics achieve the same goal by "cleansing" with laxatives, while others exercise obsessively until they burn all the calories ingested.

Frequently, they switch between these methods of "cleansing" or even combine them. Bulimics do not desire these activities, which are *forced* on them, since this is the only way for them to have it all – to overeat and stay thin at the same time.

Another important factor, serotonin, also participates in this murky, inventive bulimic chaos, closing the bulimic circle.

Serotonin is a chemical in the brain similar to a hormone. It belongs to a group of neurotransmitters, chemical mediators in the transport of stimuli among brain cells (neurons). Neurotransmitters produce feelings and moods, making you act in a certain way and sealing your lifestyle. Your thoughts and beliefs, the foods you eat, and the amount of physical activity you engage in, in turn affect levels of neurotransmitters in the brain, as well as your emotions.

In bulimia, serotonin is the most important neurotransmitter, while two others, noradrenalin and dopamine are significant as well.

The level of serotonin in the brain for the most part determines the course and intensity of the bulimic disorder. Having the opposite effect of powerful insulin, it slows down the "addiction" to carbohydrates, reducing the emotional instability and irritability of the patient.

Unlike insulin, serotonin is a chemical with only positive physical and emotional effects on the human body.

When its levels in the brain are normal and stable, serotonin generates its three most important positive effects:

1. Creating a feeling of *fullness,*

2. Having a *calming and relaxing effect,*

3. Creating a feeling of *satisfaction* (happiness hormone).

A lower level of serotonin in the brain causes the opposite effects – a feeling of hunger, nervousness, and anxiety in addition to feelings of despair and dismay, which are typical of depression.

Depression is also a result of a lower serotonin level.

Few people have a stable, high level of serotonin in the brain. Not many of us are lucky enough to remain calm in the face of life's problems, enjoying everything we do. Most people have insufficient amounts of serotonin in the brain, living in stress and anxiety, unaware of what peace and satisfaction feel like. *Depression* is their fate, and when they try to achieve a few moments of joy and satisfaction, they usually develop different addictions (nicotine, sugar, alcohol, narcotics, and the like). This happens because addictive substances create a feeling of satisfaction precisely by modifying the existing levels of neurotransmitters in the brain.

Every person has their own typical level of serotonin, having developed a certain pattern of thought, mood, and behavior over the years, supporting and maintaining this level of serotonin. Genetics plays a significant role in forming specific levels of serotonin, as well as acquired mental attitudes (family values, school, surroundings, work, and relationships with others), food, behavior, and habits.

This is why some people are naturally stable, happy, and satisfied with their lives, while others are mostly depressed and unhappy. Depressed people maintain their chemical imbalance in the brain precisely with their depressive lifestyle, which develops over time into a new chemical state that does not make them happy, but is something they are used to and feel comfortable with.

This is precisely the case with bulimics. They are depressed and unhappy, and when life surprises them with a positive event, they are unable to feel comfortable with happy feelings, and immediately look for (and find) a reason to return to their state of depression.

American scientists from the Massachusetts Institute of Technology were the first to claim, back in the late seventies, that neurotransmitter levels in the brain can be significantly influenced by certain ingredients in every single meal. They discovered that only one meal rich in proteins increases the level of the neurotransmitter noradrenalin in the brain. This leads to better concentration and decisiveness, increasing the ability to reach decisions under stress.

A meal rich in carbohydrates increases the level of serotonin in the brain, resulting in a feeling of relaxation and calm.

Recent discoveries indicate a number of nutrients and food

supplements that help the brain produce its own "medicine".

Insulin and serotonin seesaw game

Insulin in the blood and serotonin in the brain are connected in an unusual way – their concentrations are always diametrically opposed in the system, or as I like to put it – they are playing on a seesaw.

I will explain this on the example of bulimia.

As you know by now, when you embark on an eating binge and consume a large amount of carbohydrates, your blood sugar level surges. Your pancreas then excretes a lot of insulin, which in turn brings the blood glucose level below the normal range. Since the level of serotonin in the brain corresponds to the amount of sugar in blood, a large amount of insulin and a sudden drop of glucose in blood will result in a sudden drop in serotonin levels in the brain. In other words, an increase of insulin in blood causes a drop in serotonin levels in the brain – just like a seesaw game.

Due to the onset of functional hypoglycemia, you will feel a craving for carbohydrates again, along with a whole spectrum of adverse effects caused by the lowered serotonin – anxiety, dissatisfaction and depression. You will be unable to feel full, regardless of the amount of food you consume.

In this situation, bulimic binges will surely continue, and bulimia will progress.

On the other hand, if you do not embark on an eating binge with carbohydrates, but eat a meal consisting exclusively of proteins and fats (bacon and eggs), your blood sugar level will remain unchanged, within the normal range (since only carbohydrates turn into glucose, while proteins and fats do not). The pancreas will not receive a stimulus to release insulin into the blood. The level of insulin in the blood will then be insignificant, while serotonin levels in the brain will grow to normal levels, and you will feel the positive effects of an increase in serotonin – fullness, calm, and satisfaction.

This is precisely the effect that I use in the diet plan during the first 15 days. It will immediately result in no more binge eating and a withdrawal of addiction to carbohydrates in a simple – physiological manner. In this period, you will be able to eat certain food combinations until you are full (based on the menu provided), and enjoy wonderful effects of high serotonin. At the same time you will easily avoid all the negative effects of insulin.

This is how the bulimic metabolic imbalance caused by binge eating will begin to change and slowly return back to balance. Simultaneously, both your physical and psychological condition will change for the better (with a stable, high level of serotonin).

From an always hungry, depressive person, you will turn into a calm and happy one, who feels full after moderate and healthy meals.

Young women become bulimic due to their obsessive desire to become thinner and more beautiful. Their main drive and motive is the fear of weight gain.

A bulimic's logic is this – "whatever enters the system must come out as soon as possible". They are painfully consistent in this.

Bulimics usually know enough about nutrients and diet, and would like to eat moderate and healthy meals. They are unable to do this since their daily suppression of negative emotions with chocolate and other sweets takes them to a vicious and unwanted metabolic addiction – first into overeating and then into vomiting – a collateral damage of sorts that they endure and meticulously perform in order to stay slim.

Bulimics live an imaginary, idealistic life, permitting themselves to eat everything they want in unlimited quantities, enjoying "forbidden" foods to the maximum, and using it as doping. They remain slim (or in their minds, beautiful and desirable), accepting constant vomiting as a price to pay for it. In this, they have completely overlooked the onset of a dangerous addiction to carbohydrates in the form of uncontrollable binge eating. This lack of control was not something they planned or desired. It came as a result of their own naiveté, having underestimated the physiology and wisdom of their bodies. They developed a bulimic disorder as an unplanned companion to their childish dream of happiness. If you are wondering which bulimic wish can become reality without being detrimental to the health, here is my answer.

Bulimics could eat anything they want and enjoy food without feeling fear or guilt if they learn to determine the correct healthy structure and size of their meals.

Bulimics can become and remain slim if they behave in accordance with the proper daily structure.

Bulimics can live a healthy, happy, and successful life once they learn to fulfill their basic needs in life in a healthy and positive manner.

Below, I will explain a detailed diet plan according to the Overcoming Bulimia Program.

Diet plan, stage one

Seven days

The aim of the first stage of overcoming bulimia is to stop the obsessive desire for carbohydrates, eliminating binge eating, which will in turn automatically eliminate vomiting.

Metabolic processes will reverse then and return to its original balance, which was disrupted by the disease.

Since the onset of "addiction" to carbohydrates is primarily caused by the hormone insulin, the same hormone will enable the withdrawal of this "addiction".

This is why I have to repeat what you already know – whenever there is excess insulin in the blood, a strong feeling of hunger occurs, and the food ingested is quickly turned into body fat, while fat created earlier cannot be burned and eliminated from the system.

On the other hand, when no insulin is found in the blood or there is very little of it (glycemia being at normal levels), a craving for carbohydrates will not occur, food will not be transformed into fat and the excess fat deposits will easily be burned and eliminated from the system.

This is why the main goal of the diet in the first seven days is to *reduce the amount of insulin in the blood* as much as possible and to prevent its excretion from the pancreas. The blood will be free from insulin and its addictive, fattening effects.

Managing the release of insulin from the pancreas into the blood can only be achieved by controlling the amounts and types of carbohydrates ingested with food.

I want to remind you once again, as this is crucial, that in the process of digestion only carbohydrates can turn into sugar (glucose), which is why only they can raise the level of glucose in the blood, stimulating the pancreas to release insulin into the blood. Fats and proteins, on the other hand, never turn to glucose with digestion, and their intake will not influence the level of glucose in blood, while the pancreas will not be stimulated to release insulin.

In other words, a lot of carbohydrates in a meal will mean a lot of insulin in the blood, while a small amount of carbohydrates will result in less insulin in the blood. *Accordingly, no carbohydrates in a meal mean no insulin in the blood.*

Now you can understand why there will be practically no carbohydrates in your meals in the first seven days, or very few. You will be sending your pancreas on a well-deserved "vacation", having been overworked in your bulimia, excreting huge amounts of insulin after every eating binge with carbohydrates.

During the first 7 days, you will eat 3 healthy and abundant meals every day. Do not worry, you will ingest enough adequate nutrients to fulfill all your physical needs. I can guarantee that you will feel full and happy, bursting with energy, while your craving for carbohydrates will disappear after only 24 hours. At the same time, now that you know that without insulin the food ingested cannot be transformed into fat in the body, your fear of weight gain will disappear, making vomiting completely unnecessary. There is a bonus, too – these meals are usually followed by a slight weight loss (if you have excess fat deposits), as you now know that fat deposits are burned only when there is no insulin in the blood. So, during the first 7 days you will be eating plenty of healthy foods, with a minimum carbohydrate content in your meals. At the end of stage one, your craving for carbohydrates will disappear entirely. You could also lose 1 to 2 kg of fat from your system, while your muscular mass will remain untouched. The food you will eat in the first stage will be typical and familiar food that you have eaten previously, the difference being that the meals will be composed differently, since the carbohydrates have been temporarily left out.

The amounts of food have not been strictly determined – you can eat until you are full. There is no need to be afraid of this, since the lack of insulin in the blood quickly creates a feeling of fullness, while all extra food that is not used by the body will be discharged through the intestines and bladder.

Below are important remarks you must read and understand in the first stage, and apply strictly.

Stage one – important remarks
1. You must strictly comply with the prescribed menu.
Do not add or eat any food not listed on the menu.
Cake and other sweets are strictly forbidden – later in the program you will receive recipes for the sweets that are permitted. It is possible to reverse the order of meals in a day (lunch and dinner or breakfast and dinner).
2. Make sure you do not consume any foods containing even the smallest amounts of sugar (sucrose) or any type of flour during the first 7 days. When purchasing food, read the list of ingredients carefully, since sugar is oftentimes added in different forms (all words ending with –ose are sugars like sucrose, lactose, maltose, glucose, fructose, dextrose, etc.).

3. Calories are not counted in this program. You may eat as much of these foods, whose amount is not limited in the menu supplied, as is necessary to become full.

4. Do not skip meals or eat anything between meals.

If you have eaten enough during a meal, you will not feel any need for additional snacking between meals.

5. I recommend that 5 to 7 hours pass between meals (for instance – breakfast at 8 AM, lunch at 1 PM and dinner at 7 PM).

After 7 PM it is recommended that you do not eat anything, but if you do feel hungry, you can eat any of the foods permitted that day.

6. In regards to artificial sweeteners, all those not containing carbohydrates (saccharine (Natreen), aspartame, cyclamate, sorbitol) are permitted, but in very small amounts.

I recommend sweetening beverages with sucralose, fructose (fruit sugar) and Stevia (ground leaves of the *Stevia rebaudiana* plant), as they are natural and have an exceptionally low glycemic index.

Lemonade, coffee, or tea sweetened with natural sweeteners can be consumed throughout the day. You can also drink sugar-free beverages (Cola Light and others), but not excessive amounts.

7. Food can be salted as usual and seasoned with all spices you prefer (except when directed otherwise by your doctor).

8. With regard to fat, for cooking and seasoning salads, use exclusively plant oils (particularly extra virgin olive oil, corn germ oil, sesame and peanut oil, squash and sunflower oil) due to their high content of beneficial unsaturated fatty acids.

9. Raw vegetables in salads are very important for their high content in vitamins and minerals; they are also beneficial for digestion due to the high content of ballast materials - cellulose fibers.

This is why it is advisable to consume large amounts of salads.

10. In the first stage it is necessary to consume *one lemon* daily in the form of fresh-squeezed lemonade (without sugar,

sweetened artificially).

11. A lot of liquids are recommended, mainly bottled spring water. It is necessary to drink 8 to 10 glasses of water (two liters) daily, in the form of water, tea, fresh-squeezed lemonade or diet beverages.

Fruit juices of any kind are not permitted.

12. A high dosage of multivitamin and mineral pills must be taken every day (I recommend time-release pills – one in the morning after breakfast and one in the evening after dinner).

First stage of the diet plan – seven-day menu

DAY ONE
Breakfast
0.5 l of lemonade from a fresh-squeezed lemon
Three-egg omelet with 3 slices of turkey or prosciutto
3 green olives, cucumber, radishes
Coffee or tea

Lunch
Baked or cooked chicken (any desired amount)
Lettuce (only the green leaves) seasoned with apple vinegar and corn germ oil or olive oil
Artificially sweetened soda of choice
Coffee or tea

Dinner
Chicken or turkey breast salami (any desired amount)
100 g of hard cheese
3 green olives, cucumber, radishes
Mineral water, coffee or tea

DAY TWO
Breakfast
0.5 l of lemonade from a fresh-squeezed lemon

Turkey hot dog with mustard (any desired amount)
3 green olives, cucumber, radishes
Coffee or tea

Lunch
Fish, calamari or shrimp (any desired amount) prepared as
desired (except fried)
Lettuce (only the green leaves) seasoned with apple vinegar
and olive oil
Artificially sweetened soda of choice
Coffee or tea

Dinner
Omelet – one whole egg and three egg whites
3 tablespoons of fresh fat-free cheese
3 green olives, cucumber, radishes
Mineral water, coffee or tea

DAY THREE
Breakfast
0.5 l of lemonade from a fresh-squeezed lemon
Ham (any desired amount), 100 g of hard cheese
3 green olives, cucumber, radishes
Coffee or tea with a replacement sweetener

Lunch
Baby beef or turkey patties (any desired amount)
Lettuce (only the green leaves) seasoned with apple vinegar
and corn germ oil
Artificially sweetened soda of choice

Dinner
Turkey hot dog with mustard (any desired amount)
3 green olives, cucumber, radishes
Mineral water, coffee or tea

DAY FOUR
Breakfast
0.5 l of lemonade from a fresh-squeezed lemon
Three-egg omelet with ham and parmesan cheese
3 green olives, cucumber, radishes
Coffee or tea

Lunch
A large steak - your choice of meat (grilled or pan grilled)
Lettuce (only the green leaves) seasoned with apple vinegar
and corn germ oil
Artificially sweetened soda of choice

Dinner
Chicken salami, 100 g of hard cheese
3 green olives, cucumber, radishes
Mineral water, coffee or tea

DAY FIVE
Breakfast
0.5 l of lemonade from a fresh-squeezed lemon
Two hard-boiled eggs with ham and 100 g of hard cheese
3 green olives, cucumber, radishes
Coffee or tea

Lunch
Chicken liver with sour cream (3 teaspoons)
150 g of button mushrooms, sautéed on olive oil
Lettuce
Artificially sweetened soda of choice

Dinner
Canned sardines or tuna with lemon
3 green olives, cucumber, radishes
Mineral water, coffee or tea

DAY SIX
Breakfast
0.5 l of lemonade from a fresh-squeezed lemon
Omelet with parmesan
3 green olives, cucumber, radishes
Coffee or tea

Lunch
Fish, calamari or shrimp (prepared as desired)
Spinach purée (200 g) with 3 teaspoons of sour cream
Lettuce
Artificially sweetened soda of choice

Dinner
Ham (any desired amount), 100 g of hard cheese
3 green olives, cucumber, radishes
Mineral water, coffee or tea

DAY SEVEN
Breakfast
0.5 l of lemonade from a fresh-squeezed lemon
Turkey hot-dogs with mustard
3 green olives, cucumber, radishes
Coffee or tea

Lunch
1 serving of clear soup
Boiled baby beef with mustard and horseradish
150 g of steamed cauliflower
Lettuce
Artificially sweetened soda of choice
Coffee or tea

Dinner
Omelet from 4 egg whites
Steamed broccoli

3 green olives, cucumber, radishes
Mineral water, coffee or tea

In the first stage of the diet plan you will eat in a different manner but will also live a new life. You must keep your journal every day, as a reminder of your short-term and long-term plans in life, as a means of controlling your daily activities, and for an intimate emotional confession at day's end.

The journal will become your best friend and advisor, a faithful supporter on the road to regaining your health.

You must start every day with a careful plan for proper structure of your day, a structure that will give you enough time for all activities that matter to you, and optimum fulfillment of all your needs in life that we discussed earlier.

A properly structured day will make you calm and happy, even in the most stressful activities, since you will be ready, having planned them. The positive emotions that you will feel throughout the day will influence all your activities, and serotonin, as the master of your emotions and moods, will play the most significant role in this. Gradually, you will experience how its different levels in the brain make all the difference between a life with depression (and with bulimia) and a happy (and healthy) life.

In order to continually maintain serotonin at a high level, and to strengthen your muscles and heart, you must engage in *aerobic training* every day for 30 to 45 minutes.

Aerobic exercise is *endurance training*, which raises the level of serotonin, as opposed to anaerobic training, which focuses on developing strength (weightlifting), during which the level of serotonin does not change.

Aerobic training includes any movement of medium intensity for at least 30 continual minutes, like speed walking, jogging, swimming, biking, rollerblading, dancing, and exercising on aerobic equipment like a treadmill, stepper, exercise bicycle, orbitrek, rowing machine, and the like.

After only 30 minutes the level of serotonin increases significantly, and along with it the feeling of calm and self-confidence. Another advantage of this kind of training is the release of endorphins in the brain, a chemical substance which creates a feeling of happiness.

All these chemicals will bring you the very needed feeling of satisfaction and calm, sweeping away your depression as if it had never been there.

After seven days in the Program, you will be able to live a mostly healthy life – a life without bulimia, without investing a special effort or strain.

Here is a summary of the first stage of the program–healthy diet, no starving, moderate exercise, slim figure, no feeling of hunger, feelings of calm and satisfaction.

Cravings for sweet foods and for overeating have vanished.

Your fear of gaining weight has disappeared again, and there is no more reason to think about vomiting. The few kilograms that you have lost without effort in a week are the best evidence of the fact that you can maintain your weight easily and in a healthy manner by controlling insulin, instead of by vomiting, like before. You now realize that fat deposits are created after a meal only when combined with carbohydrates (and consequently, insulin), while their combination with proteins is harmless for weight gain, as no insulin is released then.

Thanks to serotonin, you are no longer depressed, and there is no more need to look for consolation in sweets.

You are now ready to begin enjoying your life by participating in it, not just as the unhappy observer that you used to be.

If this is the case, then let's proceed!

You are now ready for the next seven days – the second stage of the diet plan.

Diet plan, stage two

Seven days

Now that you have managed to easily and simply "calm down" your pancreas, giving it a seven-day rest, you are ready to gradually increase the amount of carbohydrates in your diet. You must bear in mind that these have to be exclusively good carbohydrates (with low glycemic indexes). It is very important that the reintroduction of carbohydrates is gradual and careful, so that your blood sugar levels do not suddenly increase after seven days, which would cause the release of insulin.

Our goal is for the pancreas to continually excrete only minimum amounts of insulin, so small as not to disrupt the metabolic system that we have just brought back to normal levels.

Healthy foods containing the lowest amounts of good carbohydrates are *vegetables*!

This is why your diet, starting with day eight, will include gradually increasing amounts of vegetables, both raw and cooked.

Vegetables, in addition to small amounts of carbohydrates (starch), also contain water, fibers, vitamins, and minerals.

Antioxidants are the most important substance in vegetables. They slow down the aging of cells, protecting the body from potential tumors, and are vital for our life and health.

Of all the different types of vegetables, *green, leafy vegetables* contain the smallest amount of carbohydrates. They are also quite rich in minerals and vitamins, and you should eat as much of them as possible. This includes lettuce, lamb's lettuce, arugula, spinach, Swiss chard, cabbage, Savoy cabbage and Brussels sprouts, green beans, and leeks.

The next group with low amounts of carbohydrates are broccoli, cauliflower, zucchini, asparagus, artichokes, radishes, tomatoes, eggplant, peppers, kohlrabi, parsley root, celery, and others.

Foods rich in starch – potatoes, rice, beans, and legumes – contain too many carbohydrates for the second stage, which is why they have been left out for now, but you will be able to enjoy them later.

In the second stage, you will eat fat-free dairy products like milk, yogurt, and fresh cheeses. You can also enjoy soy products, a good alternative to dairy – soy milk, soy yogurt, tofu, and soy cream.

The second stage allows for small, healthy snacks between meals, consisting of seeds and nuts (pumpkin and sunflower seeds, sesame and linseed seeds, walnuts, almonds, hazelnuts, and pine nuts).

All seeds and nuts contain large amounts of vitamins and minerals, as well as healthy unsaturated fats, with a low amount of carbohydrates, making them nutritious, healthy food.

Their only drawback is their high calorie count (100 grams of nuts or seeds contains about 700 calories), which is why they must be consumed in limited amounts (of about 30 grams in a single snack).

A special reward in the second stage is *chocolate*!

The healthiest type is dark chocolate with a high cocoa content and not much sugar. You can eat 8 pieces of dark chocolate each day (with a cocoa content of more than 70%) or diet chocolate, which is artificially sweetened.

Second stage of the diet plan – seven-day menu

DAY ONE
Breakfast
Organic breakfast (see Appendix for recipe)
Coffee or tea

Lunch
Chicken vegetable soup (any desired amount)
Artificially sweetened soda of choice

Dinner
Two boiled eggs, ham
Radishes, cucumbers
Mineral water, coffee or tea

DAY TWO
Breakfast
Organic breakfast (see Appendix for recipe)
Coffee or tea

Lunch
Fish, calamari or shrimp (prepared as desired, except fried)
200 g of steamed vegetables topped with soy cream
Salad of choice
Artificially sweetened soda of choice

Dinner
Two-egg omelet
Fresh mozzarella cheese – one ball (125 g)
3 green olives
1 tomato
Mineral water, coffee or tea

DAY THREE
Breakfast
0.5 l of lemonade from a fresh-squeezed lemon
Ham, 100 g of hard cheese
3 green olives, cucumber, radishes
Coffee or tea

Lunch
Baby beef sautéed in chopped onions (1 small 50 g onion)
Steamed green beans
Artificially sweetened soda of choice
Dinner
Turkey hot dogs with mustard

Fresh pepper
Mineral water, coffee or tea

DAY FOUR
Breakfast
0.5 l of lemonade from a fresh-squeezed lemon
100 g of hard cheese
Turkey breast salami
1 tomato, 1 fresh pepper
3 green olives
Coffee or tea

Lunch
Baked chicken
200 g of button mushrooms, sautéed in butter and served with sour cream
Cabbage salad
Artificially sweetened soda of choice

Dinner
Turkey hot-dogs with mustard
1 probiotic yogurt
3 green olives, radishes
Mineral water, coffee or tea

DAY FIVE
Breakfast
Organic breakfast (see Appendix for recipe)
Coffee or tea

Lunch
Grilled calamari
Grilled vegetables (of choice)
Artificially sweetened soda of choice
Dinner
Chicken breast salad (lettuce, peppers, tomato, spring onion)

Mineral water, coffee or tea

DAY SIX
Breakfast
Organic breakfast (see Appendix for recipe)
Coffee or tea

Lunch
1 serving of clear soup
Turkey steak (not fried)
Spinach purée with 3 teaspoons of sour cream
Salad of choice
Artificially sweetened soda of choice

Dinner
2 boiled eggs
Smoked turkey breast
Cabbage salad
Mineral water, coffee or tea

DAY SEVEN
Breakfast
Organic breakfast (see Appendix for recipe)
Coffee or tea

Lunch
Fish (prepared as desired, except fried)
250 g of steamed Brussels sprouts topped with tartar sauce
Lettuce, radishes, cucumbers, as desired
Artificially sweetened soda of choice

Dinner
Tanya's crêpes with diet marmalade
(3 crêpes, see Appendix for recipe)
Coffee or tea

Naturally, during this stage you must still continue to keep a journal, structure your time, and engage in aerobic exercise.

This will maintain low levels of insulin in your blood, while serotonin levels in the brain will continually remain high. This position of the "insulin and serotonin seesaw" is ideal for you, since it is precisely this that will cure your bulimia.

These are the two main conditions allowing you to have a life without symptoms of bulimia, a life without binge eating, without vomiting, and without depression.

If you have been complying strictly with all the instructions in the first and second stages of the program, you should be feeling calm, full, and satisfied after the first fourteen days, bursting with energy and enthusiasm.

By now, bulimia should be gone without a trace.

Diet plan - stage three

A diet based on the glycemic index

Fourteen days have passed during the first and second stages of your new diet and different lifestyle. You have managed to escape from the circle of addictive overeating of carbohydrates, having learned that when you structure your meals, you can control not only your feeling of hunger, but also your moods.

This is how you have achieved your first goal – by stopping your "addictive" overeating and depression.

The next goal you face is maintaining a proper and healthy diet from now on. This will only be possible if you fully control your insulin, by managing to keep it at low or moderate levels all the time.

You have experienced now that low insulin levels in the blood does not evoke hunger or cravings for carbohydrates. Along with your low insulin levels, your serotonin levels are always high (seesaw rule), which guarantees your good mood and permanently keeps depression at bay.

The time has come, and it must be your desire by now, to begin eating normal, mixed meals with all kinds of food (proteins, fats, and carbohydrates).

But the main issue here is whether you will relapse back into your old state of addiction and bulimia by eating large amounts of carbohydrates, which will again pump up the levels of insulin in your blood.

My answer is – do not worry, because it will not happen. I will teach you how to eat carbohydrates and keep insulin under control at the same time. I will also show you how and when to eat fats, which types, and in what combinations.

This third stage of the diet is the most important of all, since its rules are basic rules for a varied, healthy diet as well, that you will have to stick to for the rest of your life, if you do not want to relapse back into the "addiction" – overeating and bulimia. What is the most important thing in stage three?

The most important issue is to understand, remember, and use the term glycemic index, as it is precisely this that is protecting you from a relapse into bulimia.

The carbohydrate glycemic index must become your most important companion and friend when planning your meals. It will enable you to eat good carbohydrates without adverse effects, and it will indicate how much insulin is then released into your bloodstream after a meal.

You must, however, remember to recognize the alarm - "bad" carbohydrates led you to bulimia before, and they can push you back in again.

Remember once again which foods you ate in large amounts most frequently during your eating binges - these were sugar and white flour in the form of cake, creams, cookies, ice cream, chocolate, sweet or salty pastry, bread, chips, crackers, and others.

What was the common denominator in your "binge food"?

It was fat, lots of fat!

The fat you ate in your binges was precisely the worst and most harmful type of fat for your health – saturated fat from animal sources, in the form of lard, butter or cream in phyllo dough, pastry, and cake. This fat has a high level of saturated fatty acids and cholesterol, enemies of your blood vessels and heart.

Remember what would regularly happen after your binges. You had sent huge amounts of insulin into the blood, which had to turn a significant amount of fat into fat deposits - perfect circumstances for rapid weight gain. The only thing that could save you was vomiting, which is why you diligently vomited after every eating binge. You were aware that your weight gain could increase in a day if there was a delay in vomiting, or when you failed to discharge all the food from your system.

You understand now why vomiting had to be an important routine in bulimia.

"Bad" carbohydrates *in addition to fats*, your favorite bulimic combination, is precisely the worst and most dangerous combination.

Cross them out forever.

In other words, "bad" carbohydrates (particularly sugar and white flour), as well as their combination with fats, are off limits for you forever!

If it is any consolation, "bad" carbohydrates are not only damaging for your health, but for the health of everyone else as well. In addition to being fattening, they lead to diabetes, cardiovascular complications, and brain diseases.

Bear in mind that only 120 years ago, industrially processed carbohydrates like sugar and white flour did not exist at all. People ate natural foods (honey, maple syrup, wholegrain flour), while small quantities of crystal sugar used to be sold only in pharmacies. If all those people managed to live normal lives, so will you.

Let us now take a look at the good carbohydrates. They include all natural, non-processed plant foods, the way they exist in nature. Good carbohydrates include whole (unprocessed) grains, vegetables, legumes, beans, fresh fruit, seeds, and nuts. All these natural ingredients abound in vitamins, minerals, and dietary fibers.

Dietary fibers
Dietary fibers are essential for proper nutrition. Fibers are found only in plant foods, while foods from animal sources (meat, fish, eggs, dairy products) do not have them.
Fibers are indigestible portions of plants like grains, vegetables, fruits, seeds, and nuts, which are not broken down or absorbed during digestion; they only pass through the intestines. In doing so they have a beneficial effect on the intestinal lining and peristalsis. The most important components of fibers are cellulose, hemicellulose, pectin and lignin.
This is why healthy foods must include dietary fibers.
Dietary fibers have the ability to bind water molecules, therefore increasing the basic food mass passing through the intestines. This is why fibers are also referred to as ballast materials, as they are the main cleansers of the intestinal tract. Their mass increases intestinal peristalsis (movement), ensuring regular stools.
Dietary fibers slow down food digestion. Food rich in fibers must be digested for a long time by our system, which is why carbohydrates turn to sugar very slowly in the presence of fibers. Glycemia increases slowly and moderately from fiber-rich foods. The pancreas reacts to the slow growth of glycemia by not releasing much insulin, and when the level of insulin in the blood is low, its fattening effects are minor, almost imperceptible.
This is why fibers lower the glycemic index of foods ingested at the same time.
Fibers also bind with some fats from food, thus reducing the absorption of cholesterol in the blood, which is why they are also useful for lowering cholesterol.
All of the above points to the fact that the consumption of sufficient amounts of plant fibers indicates a proper and healthy diet. If you regularly eat plant foods rich in fiber with your five daily meals, you will feel full for a longer time and system

detoxicification will be more efficient. Moreover, this food has low energy values and therefore does not cause weight gain.

Ideally, the daily amounts of fiber to be consumed are approximately 25 grams (for women) and 35 grams (for men), spread over several meals, which is sufficient to ensure all their beneficial effects. This is possible only with daily consumption of wholegrain, unprocessed plant foods.

The industrial refining (purifying, bleaching) of grains, which started some 100 years ago, turned into a real hazard for human health, causing cardiovascular diseases, heart attacks, and strokes, as well as the epidemics of obesity and diabetes that have been seen in the developed world. The main goal in food refining is the elimination precisely of dietary fibers, so that the final product, such as white flour or white crystal sugar, can be manipulated more easily and added to other foods. But at the same time, they become easily digestible since their glycemic index increases several times. This is why industrially processed food without fibers (white bread, pasta, and sweets) is not filling, which quickly leads again to hunger and increased appetites. This creates conditions for a mass "addiction" to white flour and sugar, which suits the food industry perfectly in their race for profit.

Since half-cooked and ready-to-eat fast food, which is consumed the most these days, has already been "semi-digested" in the processing plant, it leaves very little debris in the intestinal tract, causing constipation. This results in debris materials and toxins remaining in the intestines for a while, preventing the body from regular cleansing and creating preconditions for the development of inflammations and tumors.

The highest amounts of fibers are found in wheat, corn and oat brans, seeds and unprocessed whole grains, in fruit (pectin in apple skin), and in green, leafy vegetables, as well as in seeds (linseed and sesame) and nuts (walnuts, almonds, hazelnuts, pistachios, peanuts), which is why all of these foods are referred to as good carbohydrates and must be consumed daily. In addition to these good carbohydrates, if you limit your intake of fats, especially saturated fats from animal sources, the benefits to your health will be even higher. In this case, insulin, even when found in the blood in moderate quantities, will not have the necessary materials for creating fat deposits in the body.

I have to emphasize once again that not all fats are bad, that fats from plant sources are crucial in small quantities for the proper functioning of the system, and for metabolizing fat-soluble vitamins (vitamins A, D, E, and K). For these nutritional purposes, small amounts of fats from plant sources are sufficient, being healthy due to their high content of unsaturated fatty acids and their lack of cholesterol. I particularly recommend cold-pressed natural plant oils like olive, squash, corn germ, and sunflower seed oils. These oils protect the blood vessels and the heart, and participate in the synthesis of some significant hormones.

Stage three – seven-day menu

DAY ONE
Breakfast
0.5 l of lemonade from a fresh-squeezed lemon
4 wholegrain crackers with fresh, fat-free cheese
1 probiotic yogurt (0.1% fat)
Coffee or tea

Snack
Fruit (1 apple or 2 oranges or 3 tangerines)

Lunch
Clear chicken soup
Cooked chicken from the soup
Sautéed button mushrooms
Mixed salad of choice
Artificially sweetened soda of choice

Snack
1 handful of nuts (approximately 30 g)

Dinner
1 serving (approximately 300 g) of a fruit salad of choice

DAY TWO
Breakfast
½ grapefruit
Two boiled eggs, ham
1 tomato, 1 fresh pepper
Tea

Snack
Fruit

Lunch
Vegetable soup
Onion-sautéed chicken liver
Salad of choice
Artificially sweetened soda of choice

Snack
30 g of almonds

Dinner
5 tablespoons of wholegrain cereal flakes topped with skim
milk

DAY THREE
Breakfast
Organic breakfast (see Appendix for recipe)
Coffee or tea

Snack
Fruit

Lunch
Cauliflower, minced meat, mozzarella cheese and egg
casserole Lettuce
Artificially sweetened soda of choice
Coffee or tea

Snack
30 g of almonds

Dinner
1 serving of soy pasta topped with (sugar-free) tomato sauce
and sprinkled with parmesan cheese
Tea

DAY FOUR
Breakfast
3 diet crêpes (see Appendix for recipe)
Coffee with milk

Snack
Fruit

Lunch
Fish of choice
Steamed Swiss chard with garlic and olive oil
Steamed wholegrain rice
Mixed salad of choice
Artificially sweetened soda of choice

Snack
30 g of almonds

Dinner
2 boiled eggs
100 g of fresh fat-free cheese
Cucumber salad

Tea

DAY FIVE
Breakfast
0.5 l of lemonade from a fresh-squeezed lemon
Turkey hot dogs with mustard
1 boiled egg
Pickles
Tea

Snack
Fruit

Lunch
Cauliflower, green beans, cheese, eggs and soy cream
casserole Lettuce
Artificially sweetened soda of choice

Snack
30 g of almonds

Dinner
Wholegrain pasta topped with tomato sauce and parmesan
cheese
Mixed salad of choice
Coffee or tea

DAY SIX
Breakfast
0.5 l of lemonade from a fresh-squeezed lemon
5 tablespoons of wholegrain cereal flakes topped with fat-free
yogurt

Snack
Fruit
Lunch

Cooked chicken breast
Steamed wholegrain rice, steamed broccoli
Mixed salad
Artificially sweetened soda of choice

Snack
30 g of sunflower seeds

Dinner
1 serving (approximately 300 g) of a fruit salad of choice

DAY SEVEN
Breakfast
0.5 l of lemonade from a fresh-squeezed lemon
2 slices of wholegrain bread
Fresh fat-free cheese, fat-free turkey salami
1 fresh pepper
1 probiotic yogurt

Snack
Fruit

Lunch
Fried fish or calamari (battered with wholegrain flour)
Steamed Swiss chard with garlic and olive oil
Salad of choice
Artificially sweetened soda of choice
Coffee or tea

Snack
Tanya's fast cake (see Appendix for recipe)

Dinner
4 turkey hot dogs
1 boiled egg, cabbage salad
1 probiotic yogurt

Let us now summarize the third stage of the diet plan.

1. You will be eating exclusively good carbohydrates in the third stage, including whole grains, lots of vegetables (in the form of side dishes and salads), beans, legumes, all types of fruit, drupes and nuts.

2. Along with good carbohydrates, you should only be eating fat-free food from animal sources (fat-free dairy products, lean meat and meat products), since animal fats contain harmful saturated fatty acids.

Fish are an exception, because they are beneficial both with fat and fat-free. Fatty fish from cold oceans (e.g. salmon and tuna) along with fatty blue fish (e.g. mackerel and pilchard) are exceptionally healthy due to their high content of good omega-3 unsaturated fatty acids, which protect the heart and blood vessels.

3. Fats from plant sources are healthy when consumed in small quantities, containing primarily good, unsaturated fatty acids.

In cooking, you should use sunflower and olive oils. As a topping for fish, vegetables, and salads, use extra virgin olive oil, as well as squash, sesame, or corn germ oil, and when needed, soy cream.

4. In the third stage you should eat five meals daily – breakfast, lunch, dinner, and two snacks, consisting of fruit or nuts.

5. Your meals must be moderate, which translates into restaurant serving size quantities.

Trust me, you will not experience extreme hunger again, because your levels of the "hunger hormone" – insulin – in your blood will never be excessive again, despite the numerous meals. Because of the moderate amount of insulin, the food you consume will be sufficient for the production of necessary energy needed every day, and will not transform into fat. As a result, your weight will remain normal. The need to induce vomiting will disappear along with your fear of gaining weight.

6. Try to develop a habit of ending dinner by 8 PM at the latest, and do not eat anything after this time, primarily because you will not need extra food, and also to give the pancreas a rest

overnight, so that it does not have to release insulin for 12 hours.

7. The diet in stage three contains menus for only one week, but once you fully understand the basic principles of a glycemic index diet, you will be able to create healthy and tasty meals with ease and satisfaction, and enjoy them without fear of weight gain. Your insulin control will transform into an automatic and routine activity over time.

8. When you analyze the stage three menu in more detail, you will realize it is quite similar to our Dalmatian cuisine, a part of the Mediterranean diet.

The Mediterranean diet has been declared the best diet for human health by the most prominent global nutrition institutions, and is an example to all countries world-wide.

9. What will be decisive for your success is whether you have managed to evoke enthusiasm, or even a passion, for this healthy diet, now that you have acquired all the necessary knowledge about it. If you have succeeded in doing so, you will never again have the urge to stuff yourself with fatty foods loaded with white flour and sugar. You will discover the subtle and wonderful tastes of natural foods, find this food far tastier, and prefer them to industrially processed or treated foods.

10. A day that begins with a breakfast consisting of wholegrain cereal mixed with a few nuts and fresh fruit, such as grated apples, will be very energizing, making you feel light and full. This breakfast will fulfill all your needs for carbohydrates in the healthiest possible way, and the low level of insulin released will not develop any urge to overeat – a moderate meal will suffice.

11. Lunch can contain fat-free proteins (fish, seafood, chicken, turkey, veal, lamb, fat-free baby beef), combined with vegetables and salads. Another option is whole grains (like brown rice) mixed with vegetables, beans, or legumes. You can eat any amount of this food, as much as you need to feel full, since this is ballast food, meaning that even large amounts have relatively few calories due to the high fiber content.

12. An ideal dinner based on the glycemic index would be a sandwich with whole-grain bread (rye is preferable), with fresh, fat-free cheese, fat-free turkey salami and LGG fat-free yogurt.

13. Ideal snacks include fruit, which can be combined with a few walnuts, almonds, or hazelnuts, while your craving for something sweet can be satisfied by fat-free fruit yogurt, which comes in a range of flavors.

14. My advice is to learn to cook under all circumstances, to begin collecting recipes, and to adapt them to meals based on the glycemic index.

16. Get to know different spices, come up with your own salad dressing mixes, and turn into an expert on vegetables, beans, legumes, and grains.

17. Fairly soon you will be able to create different, tasty, and healthy meals, which you will surprise your friends with, teaching them that it is possible to eat tasty food without ordering fast food.

Threat of relapse into bulimia

A number of days have passed.
We are now at the end of a successful journey.
You are new persons now – calm, happy, successful, and healthy.
You have reason to be proud of yourselves.

But how does life evolve from here? How do you maintain this new life, which you have obtained with such effort?
There is no more depression to be dealt with.
There is no more overeating that throws you into despair.
I agree. It is gone.
But something else is still here.
Something important is still here, lurking in the shadows.
Something dangerous and vicious.

Your old "loser" mental program! Your previous negative mindset!

They are still here, close by. Lurking and waiting for their chance to return. To win you over with old problems and previous habits.

The danger that your previous "loser" pattern will return is still present. It will diminish over time, but it will be around for a while to come.

Its return must be prevented. It should not be given a single chance. Never again.

Today, you are not victims. Now you are winners.

Your main goal is to keep things this way.

Winners – forever.

You must monitor your thoughts and your feelings attentively, this is crucial.

Are you still in a positive mindset and full of optimism?

As long as you are, and you continue to live according to the winning principles of the Program, everything will be fine – your thoughts, emotions, and behavior; your diet and your results. And accordingly, your weight. You will attain your normal weight value and maintain it without effort.

Your health and physical condition will be wonderful; your psychological state will be stable and full of enthusiasm.

I know that everything will be perfectly fine as long as your life is smooth and successful.

As long as you are calm and satisfied, it is easy and simple to generate pleasant thoughts, to happily consume food that does not create fat deposits, to enjoy exercise and work.

But occasionally, hard days will come, filled with tiresome jobs, anxiety, disappointments, and stress.

This will surely occur. No life is always coated in pink.

So be ready. Despite your following the Program regularly, occasionally you will feel strong cravings for your favorite foods – sweet and fatty.

What then? How do you cope with that?

It is precisely such stressful days that represent a *danger* for you and your future.

You must be prepared when such days occur. If you are not ready, your past will use this opportunity to return to power. Your previous emotions will surface and could overpower you. You could, once again, start believing that something is wrong with you, which is why failures occur, that life is too hard and the future too dark and uncertain . . .

All these negative thoughts will produce your previous negative emotions, just like on a factory conveyor belt. They will evoke old behavior programs, in a well-known pattern. These programs will jump at the opportunity to dominate the subconscious mind again, to resume the positions they were stripped from. They will try to eliminate and destroy all your new, fresh thoughts, all the feelings and habits you have patiently nurtured in your subconscious mind that turned your poor bulimic life into a successful and winning one.

So beware!

Your new, positive mental programs are like young, fragile, brand-new plants. They can easily be broken, pulled out, and destroyed.

Weeds overgrow easily then.

So reach a decision and assume control permanently.

Assume control for your entire future!

You must learn to recognize the *warning signs* on time, alerting you that you are only a step away from returning to your previous mindset and habits.

The most significant warning sign of imminent danger is a sudden onset of *depressive moods*, expressed by *anxiety, moroseness and dissatisfaction*. Depression will immediately be followed by an *irresistible craving for sweet food*, and you will find yourself only a step away from relapse into bulimia.

This attack of intense hunger and craving for sweets is the best sign that the old, negative thoughts and emotions, followed by an addiction to carbohydrates, are trying to return and dominate your mindset.

You must *recognize* this situation in the start, and react immediately, decisively, and without hesitation.

Turn to your life energy, feel its power and protection, and renew your vows of self-acceptance. Show understanding and love for yourself, more than ever before.

Then think well about the possible *reasons* that led you to this negative mood. Analyze and recognize the immediate *cause that led to your change in mood* – it is always a recent event related to *a relationship that is important to us.*

Talk to yourself, show yourself love, understanding, and care. Ask your inner child – "Honey, how may I help you? Are you angry, hurt, sad or desperate? What would you like to do to feel better? Say it out loud, get all the negative emotions out! Do not keep quiet and suffer ever again! Cry if you feel like crying, scream, yell, reproach, knowing I am beside you, aware that I love you unconditionally and that you will never be alone again."

In difficult times, your inner child must know that it is loved and not alone.

Do not wait for help and a solution to be provided by the outside world. Now, with your life energy in your heart, you are your own support and power. It makes a huge difference, trust me.

As soon as you manage to calm your "boiling" emotions, and once they diminish and become less intense, you are on solid ground, and can rest assured that you have prevented a relapse back into bulimia.

All this reasoning will lose power and strength over you. It will be defeated by the energy generated with renewed, positive thoughts.

With a lot of care and patience, accept everything that is happening, because that is life. Ugly and painful emotions will change and result in positive solutions, as long as you trust your life energy and as long as you love and support yourself. When your thoughts are clear and solutions are found, emotions calm down on their own.

Then, turn to the Program with even more dedication.

It is always there for you, ready and capable of saving you from your cunning old enemy.

The Overcoming Bulimia Program is your strongest weapon against the threatening danger of relapse.

For as long as you live according to the program, you will live in harmony with your life energy. You will think as a winner, feel like a winner, and your life will develop accordingly – into a successful, happy, and joyful one.

With winning, positive thoughts, all your problems in life, every anxiety you feel and each fear of failure will be simpler and easier to resolve.

Once you notice and feel that your old thoughts are trying to return, react immediately. Love yourselves, defend yourselves and win!

Just as the Program taught you to.

Here is a typical example.

Iva, a young woman who has lived a happy and healthy life without bulimia for the last three years, returned home one winter evening from the university particularly tired, nervous, and in a bad mood. It had been a bad day. She had gotten bad results on an important test and received unfounded criticism from an authority figure.

She entered her small, warm apartment, and suddenly felt a surge of craving for something tasty and sweet. Anything that could get her mind away from the sorrow, that would give her peace and quiet.

Iva was trying hard to resist the temptation, but the tempting images were dancing persistently before her eyes. She wants to sit in her favorite couch, knowing that relaxation and happiness were more intense and came faster with a tasty chocolate cake and perhaps something else forgotten in her freezer.

She threw her coat on the floor, and as if sleepwalking, walked toward her refrigerator.

But her warning signals turned on immediately!

Tempting bulimic thoughts and images had turned into an automatic warning in her mind.

Iva had become well aware of this – they were her previous, "loser" habits trying to return. If she gave in, she would go down together with them, back into bulimia and despair.

Suddenly, she was fully aware of the moment.

She stopped, knowing she must think this through. She had to change her train of thought, understand, and change her feelings.

Slowly, she went through her entire day in her mind, aware that she had to find the cause of her bad mood.

She looked for a deeper reason for her dissatisfaction. Her answer came as a shadow – so typical, she had again felt insecure and incompetent, and everyone else seemed to be better than her. Again, just like before, when nothing was good enough for her father. When criticism and lecturing was all he would give her, at a time when she needed his understanding, his acceptance, his unconditional love.

She remembered, everything had started that morning with an uncomfortable debate with a fellow student over their joint project, which Iva had completed pretty much on her own. The assistant professor had complimented her partner. She felt nervous in the afternoon during her test, making mistakes, although she knew all the answers.

She realized that negative feelings were dragging her back to her old life, so familiar, but one she never wanted to experience again – the life of bulimia and the horrific addiction to sweet foods.

She recognized the danger and decided to react calmly!

She consciously accepted, analyzed, and understood all the thoughts that had made her miserable that day. Then, having realized how predictable and superficial they were, she decisively turned them into the opposite – positive thoughts.

No, she was no longer that scared and insecure girl dependent on her father's love. Now she was an adult, a mature young woman, sure of herself and her values. Now she was a person surrounded with love from her life energy. For some time now she had been calm in accepting everything life brought her way, and sufficiently wise to protect herself in every situation. She realized immediately which events that day had evoked painful memories, aware that there was no realistic basis for them to affect her.

She had problems in life, so what! She knew this would happen occasionally. She was determined to resolve them the best she could as if nothing had happened. Everything would be fine again.

She consciously kept these positive thoughts on her mind. Iva repeated them like a magic formula, recording them in her consciousness, until she felt a clear change in her mood, with new, calm feelings.

She calmly opened the refrigerator and took out the cheese, turkey salami, yogurt, and lettuce. Wholegrain bread with seeds was already on the table, and like on so many evenings before, Iva began looking forward to her rich, healthy sandwich, and later a banana while watching her favorite show.

One dangerous day had a happy ending . . .

If Iva could do this, so can you.

Feel free to choose your thoughts. When you harmonize them with your life energy, they will immediately become positive – just as the Program has taught you.

This is the only way to successfully push away your old habits and to keep them at bay forever.

There is a different garden in your subconscious mind now – one full of sun and flowers. You have to protect and guard it from possible intruders. Create an insurmountable wall around it, constructed with valuable memories from your new life. And then, take a deep breath, smile, and relax.

Intense hunger will always disappear along with the

disappearance of negative thoughts that had previously upset your calm life.

Remember, you are not alone. Now you determine your rules of life and decide where you want life to take you.

This provides you with the freedom to calmly and wisely reach all kinds of decisions, like the one that at the next family reunion you would calmly enjoy everything - the company, the conversations, and the food. You can be calm knowing you will not be eating as a victim of addiction, but as a winner who believes in herself and her decisions.

That evening you will eat everything, and will not obsess about food.

The next day, you will go back to your program, and live the next *two days* according to the principles of the first stage - without carbohydrates. This will calm down your pancreas and lower the insulin levels in your blood. The excess carbohydrates will be burned, and everything will be fine again – you will not gain a single gram.

You will continue with your diet as usual – taking into account the glycemic index.

Naturally, these "planned feasts" should not be frequent, what matters is that they are possible and that they do not throw you back into bulimia's path.

They cannot, because you know the magic formula now. You know why you used to be a bulimic and are aware of how to prevent and keep its relapse at bay.

If you do make unplanned mistakes sometimes, by giving in and overeating carbohydrates due to anxiety or a similar feeling, it is important to bear in mind that nothing terrible happened that cannot be fixed.

The worst possible outcome would be to panic, to give up and renounce the whole Program. A relapse back into bulimia would then be unavoidable.

Therefore, stay calm.

If you make mistakes occasionally, so what? Winners never give up. Only losers do.
Winners learn from their mistakes, and start from scratch again.

For as long as you live according to the Program, your weight will be normal, with possible very minor fluctuations (within a range of 2 kg more or less).
It will be easy for you to maintain your normal weight if you consume only the amount of carbohydrates that your body can break down without having to create fat deposits from them.
The basis of your diet will still be vegetables, lean meat, fish, fat-free dairy products, fruit, grains, beans, legumes, seeds, and nuts.
Now you know that life according to the Program is the only healthy solution for overcoming bulimia. It is your only ticket to success.

The Overcoming Bulimia Program will be useful for anyone who understands it, trusts it, and happily walks down its path.

APPENDIX
RECIPES FOR DIET DESSERTS

Sweet comfort

Knowing how much you are going to miss sweet foods, here is a "sweet" surprise for you: 10 recipes for desserts with an exceptionally low glycemic index.
These desserts contain no "bad" carbohydrates – there is no regular white sugar (sucrose) and no white flour in them, yet they are still sweet and tasty. But most importantly, this is precisely why they are healthy. Moreover, these desserts contain much less fat than "regular" ones. Wherever possible, fats from animal sources (necessary in regular desserts) have been replaced by those from plant sources.
Instead of regular sugar (sucrose), natural fruit sugar, or fructose, is used to make them (glycemic index 20).
A small amount of the liquid artificial sweetener Natreen (not a carbohydrate, but a chemical with a glycemic index of 0) is added to the fructose, since the combination of various sweeteners enhances the overall sweetness.
White flour is replaced by wholegrain barley flour, or with ground seeds and nuts.
These desserts will result in a very small excretion of insulin from the pancreas, since the glycemia level increases insignificantly. This means that they will not evoke a new craving for sweet foods. Consequently, they will not cause binge eating, and there will be no need to vomit.
Occasionally (1–2 times a week) you can easily eat the allowed amounts of these desserts. You can eat them without fear of weight gain, now that you know that, with no insulin in the blood, fat deposits cannot be produced in the body.

Check your weight once a week (preferably on Monday mornings) and do not pay attention to a variation of 0.5 kg. Measuring your waist will provide you with even more precise information, since regular exercise can strengthen your muscles and increase your weight, but your waist will remain as slim as before or become even slimmer.

These desserts will give you the opportunity to have a pleasant Christmas or Easter celebration with your family. Moreover, you will have the opportunity to celebrate your birthday with a cake and candles. Feel free to offer these desserts to your friends as well – they are healthy for everyone. You do not have to reveal the ingredients to them – I can guarantee they will not notice the difference.

These recipes provide you with a unique opportunity to enjoy your favorite tastes. I want you to use them wisely and prudently, not to abuse them.

Healthy breakfast
Since breakfast provides the body with its initial energy for the day, it must be a quality meal and should not be missed. I advise the organic breakfast as often as possible (after the first 15 days, you can enjoy it every day), as it consists of a whole range of natural foods, providing your body with a multitude of valuable ingredients. It is exceptionally tasty and filling. Its sweet taste fully satisfies any craving for sweet foods, which will not reappear later in the course of the day. You can purchase the ingredients in health food specialty stores.

Organic breakfast
Ingredients for the organic mix
Wholegrain wheat flakes – 100 g
Wholegrain rye flakes – 100 g

Wholegrain oat flakes – 100 g
Wholegrain barley flakes – 100 g
Wholegrain rice flakes – 100 g
Wheat and oat bran – 200 g total
Wheat and oat germ – 200 g total
Linseed seed (ground) – 200 g
Sesame seed – 200 g
Amaranth – 200 g
Dried fruit (cranberry, raisins) – 200 g total
Sunflower seed – 200 g
Walnuts – 100 g
Hazelnuts – 100 g
Almonds – 100 g

Mix all of the above ingredients and store in a large glass container with a lid.
Once you run out of the organic mix, simply remix a new one. Keep the container in a dark place at room temperature (in a cabinet).

Organic breakfast preparation
Grate a large, prewashed apple (with the skin) into a serving bowl.
Add freshly pressed juice from one grapefruit.
Add 5 tablespoons of the organic mix to this.
Mix well and let stand for 5 minutes.
Grapefruit juice can be replaced by 200 ml of soy milk or soy yogurt.

Quick diet cake
Ingredients:
- 4 eggs
- 3 tablespoons of powdered fructose
- 1 tablespoon of liquid artificial sweetener (Natreen)

- 1 cup (200 ml) of wholegrain barley flour
- 1 cup of ground sunflower
- 2 cups of ground roasted almonds (and ½ cup more for topping)
- 1 pouch of baking powder
- ½ cup of sunflower oil
- 2 (peeled) grated medium apples
- 1 cup of soy milk
- grated peel of 1 lemon
- 1 teaspoon of lemon aroma (concentrate)
- 5 tablespoons of apricot marmalade for topping

Preparation:
Beat the eggs and both sweeteners with an electric mixer, then gradually add the remaining ingredients (except the marmalade) in the above order and mix well.
Pour the mixture into a medium-sized baking pan (lined with parchment paper).

Bake for about 20 minutes at 180°C.

While still hot, top with the diet marmalade and sprinkle with ground almonds.
Cut the cake into 20 cubes.
After day 15 of the diet program, you can have 2 cubes of the cake daily, when you want something sweet.
Freeze the remaining cake (in two-cube servings). Defrost them at room temperature or in a microwave oven.

Diet chocolate cubes
Ingredients:
- 7 eggs
- 5 tablespoons of powdered fructose
- 1 tablespoon of liquid artificial sweetener (Natreen)

- 200 g of dark chocolate (with at least 72% of cocoa powder)
- 22 rounded tablespoons of ground roasted hazelnuts
- one pouch of baking powder
- 5 drops of rum flavor (concentrate)
- 5 tablespoons of diet currant marmalade
- 250 ml of non-dairy whipping cream
- 1 teaspoon of lemon juice
- a pinch of salt

Dough preparation:
Beat the 7 egg whites with 2 tablespoons of fructose with an electric mixer until stiff, adding lemon juice and a pinch of salt for stiffness.
In another bowl, mix 7 yolks with a tablespoon of fructose and a tablespoon of liquid artificial sweetener. Add softened chocolate (soften it in a microwave oven or a regular oven at low temperature).
Add 20 rounded tablespoons of ground hazelnuts mixed with baking powder and mix well.
Finally, carefully add the egg-white mix.

Line a medium-sized baking pan with parchment paper.
Pour the mix into the pan and bake for 15-20 minutes (depending on the pan size and dough thickness) at 180°C.

Make holes in the hot baked dough with a fork, then top with marmalade, previously diluted with two tablespoons of hot water.

Topping preparation
In a large bowl beat the non-dairy whipping cream until it turns to stiff whipped cream, and add 2 tablespoons of fructose. Mix the remaining 2 tablespoons of hazelnuts into the whipped cream.

Once the cake cools, top it with the whipped cream and store in the refrigerator until it cools well.
Cut the cake into 20 cubes.
As of your 10th day on the diet program, you can eat 3 cubes of the cake occasionally (2-3 times a week) as a meal replacement, or 1-2 cubes for a snack, along with coffee or tea.

Diet waffles
Ingredients:
- 5 eggs
- 1 dl of soy creamer
- 2 dl of sparkling water
- 2 tablespoons of cooking rum
- 4 tablespoons of powdered fructose
- 10 rounded tablespoons of ground walnuts
- 5 rounded tablespoons of wholegrain barley flour
- 100 g of coconut flour
- 1 pouch of baking powder
- grated peel from 1 large lemon

Preparation:
Beat eggs until creamy, add the creamer, sparkling water, rum, and fructose.
Mix all the dry ingredients together well in another bowl: walnuts, coconut and barley flour, baking powder, and lemon peel.
Pour the liquid mixture into the dry one, mixing constantly.
Shape waffles by pouring a serving spoon of the batter into the waffle maker.
If you do not have a waffle maker, pour small heaps of the batter into a baking pan lined with parchment paper and bake at 180°C for approximately ten minutes.
You can eat 3 waffles per day occasionally, instead of dinner,

with coffee or tea.
Freeze the other waffles, three per freezer bag.

Tanya's holiday cake

Dough ingredients:
- 70 g of organic margarine (without trans fatty acids)
- 4 eggs + 3 egg whites (leftover from the cream)
- 1 tablespoon of liquid artificial sweetener (Natreen)
- 3 tablespoons of powdered fructose
- 200 g + 2 spoons (for the mold) of ground walnuts
- 4 tablespoons of wholegrain barley flour
- 1 teaspoon of baking powder
- 3 tablespoons of roasted wheat germ
- 3 tablespoons of soy creamer
- 1 teaspoon of Nescafe diluted in 2 dl of warm soy milk to moisten the dough

Cream ingredients:
- 3 yolks, 1 egg
- 3 tablespoons of powdered fructose
- 1 tablespoon of liquid artificial sweetener (Natreen)
- 2 dl (one cup) of soy creamer
- 2 tablespoons of cooking rum
- 1 teaspoon of vanilla extract
- 3 rounded tablespoons of wholegrain barley flour
- 4 rounded tablespoons of ground walnuts
- 100 g of diet chocolate
- 125 g of organic margarine (without trans fatty acids)
- 5 dl of whipped non-dairy creamer (sugar-free)

Cake preparation:
Preheat the oven to 200°C.

Line a baking pan with parchment paper.
Beat 7 egg whites with 2 tablespoons of fructose until stiff.
In another bowl cream the margarine, add the liquid artificial sweetener and a tablespoon of fructose, then gradually beat in one yolk after another.
Once creamy, add ground walnuts, rum, creamer, coconut, barley flour, and baking powder.
Finally, carefully fold in the beaten egg whites.
Bake for 20-25 minutes in an oven heated to 200°C.

Cream preparation:
Beat 3 yolks and 1 egg well with an electric mixer.
Add the rest of the ingredients except the chocolate, margarine, and whipping cream.
Heat the mixture in a double boiler, gradually adding the chocolate, and mix continually until it thickens.
Cool the cream to room temperature.
Add the margarine into the mixture and mix well with an electric mixer.
Finally, add the whipped cream (but leave some for decorating).
Cool the cream in the refrigerator until it thickens.

Cut the cake into three parts.
Moisten each part with coffee and top with cream.
Once the cake has cooled in the refrigerator, spread the cream over all sides and decorate with whipped cream.

On special occasions (holidays, birthdays) you can eat a slice of this cake.

Diet walnut cake
Cake ingredients:
- 8 eggs
- 3 tablespoons of powdered fructose

- 1 tablespoon of liquid artificial sweetener (Natreen)
- 150 g of ground walnuts
- 5 tablespoons of wholegrain barley flour
- 1 spoon of cooking rum
- soy milk for moistening

Cream ingredients:
- 300 g of ground walnuts
- 2 dl of soy milk
- 50 g of organic margarine
- 3 tablespoons of powdered fructose
- several walnut halves for decoration

Cake preparation:
Separate all of the egg yolks from the whites.
Beat the 8 egg whites with 2 tablespoons of the fructose until stiff.
In another bowl, mix the 8 yolks with the remaining sweeteners, and beat until stiff, add the walnuts, barley flour, and rum.
Finally, fold in the beaten egg whites.
Bake for half an hour at 180°C in a cake pan lined with parchment paper.
When cool, cut the cake into 2 parts.

Cream preparation:
Boil soy milk for the cream. Add ground walnuts and fructose to the hot milk. Cook on low heat until it turns thick. Add the margarine, softened, to the cooled cream. Check to see whether the cream is sweet enough.

Once cool, moisten the cake with soy milk.
Cover the lower part of the dough with cream, and spread the remaining cream on the cake.
Decorate with walnut halves.

Cool the cake well.
On special occasions (holidays, birthdays) you can eat a slice of this cake.

Diet apple cake
Cake ingredients:
- 3 eggs
- 3 tablespoons of powdered fructose
- 1 tablespoon of liquid artificial sweetener (Natreen)
- 200 ml (1 cup) of soy milk (sugar-free)
- ½ cup of oil
- 200 g of ground walnuts
- 100 g of ground sunflower seeds
- 1 pouch of baking powder
- grated peel from 1 lemon

Filling ingredients:
- 1.5 kg of peeled, grated apples
- 2 tablespoons of powdered fructose
- 1 teaspoon of cinnamon (if desired)

The grated apples must be sautéed with fructose over low heat until softened.

Cake preparation:
Beat 3 eggs with both types of sweetener using an electric mixer, add the soy milk and oil, then the walnuts, sunflower, and baking powder. Add the lemon peel and mix well.
Line the baking pan with parchment paper.
Pour half of the dough in the pan and bake until half-baked (around 10 minutes at 200°C – until it slightly hardens).
Take out of the oven, add apple filling, cover with the remaining dough and return to the oven. Reduce the oven

temperature to 180°C and bake until done (around 30 minutes).
Sprinkle the cake while still hot with powdered fructose. Once cool, cut into 20 cubes.

You are allowed to occasionally eat 3 cubes of the cake instead of a meal – for a light dinner with coffee or tea.

Diet fruit cake
Cake ingredients:
- 200 g of diet chocolate (with fructose)
- 3 eggs
- 50 g of organic margarine
- 3 rounded tablespoons of powdered fructose
- 150 g of ground walnuts
- 1 teaspoon of baking powder
- 2 tablespoons of cooking rum

Filling ingredients:
- 12 gelatin sheets
- 500 g of ripe strawberries (or raspberries); if frozen, defrost first
- 3 tablespoons of powdered fructose
- 200 g of fresh fat-free cheese
- 5 dl of whipping cream (sugar-free) – sweetened with fructose to taste
- 125 ml of fresh-squeezed orange juice

Cake preparation:
Preheat the oven to 150°C.
At low heat melt 100 g of chocolate and margarine.
Separate the egg yolks from the whites.
Beat the egg whites until stiff.

In a separate bowl, mix the egg yolks with the fructose, beating well with an electric mixer. Add the melted margarine and chocolate, then the rum, walnuts, baking powder, and finally fold in the egg whites.
Line a 24 cm baking pan with parchment paper, and pour in the cake batter.
Bake for 45 minutes at 150°C.
Set cake aside to cool.

Filling preparation:
Soak 6 gelatin sheets in a small amount of cold water.
Wash the strawberries, remove the leaves, and mix them into a smooth mixture with the fructose and well-drained cheese.
Drain the gelatin, melt it in a small amount of warm whipping cream, then add to the strawberry and cheese mixture.
Add the remaining whipped cream.
Pour over the cooled cake in the pan, and leave in the refrigerator for one hour.
Soak the remaining gelatin in cold water, drain, and dissolve in warm orange juice. Pour over the cheese and strawberry filling. Return to the refrigerator to thicken.
Melt the remaining chocolate in a double boiler and pour into a large pan, to make a thin layer.
Separate the cake from the sides of the pan with a knife and carefully move to a serving plate.
Scrape the hardened chocolate out with a utensil and decorate the cake.

On special occasions (holidays, birthdays) you can eat a slice of this cake after lunch.

Tanya's chocolate cake
Cake ingredients:
- 7 eggs

- 1 tablespoon of liquid artificial sweetener (Natreen)
- 3.5 tablespoons of powdered fructose
- 125 g of organic margarine
- 200 g of ground walnuts
- 100 g of roasted wheat germ
- 150 g of dark chocolate (with at least 85% of cocoa powder)
- 2 tablespoons of bitter cocoa powder
- 2 tablespoons of wholegrain barley flour
- 1 pouch of baking powder

Cake preparation:
Separate the egg yolks from the whites.
Beat the 7 egg whites and 2 tablespoons of fructose until stiff.
In a separate bowl, mix the margarine, artificial sweetener, 1.5 teaspoon of fructose and 7 yolks with an electric mixer until smooth.
Add walnuts, softened chocolate, and cocoa.
Mix the barley flour with baking powder and add to the mix.
Finally, carefully fold in the beaten egg whites.
Line a baking pan with parchment paper, and pour in the batter.
Bake for approximately 45 minutes at 175°C.
Spoon out the center of the cake, leaving the bottom and sides 1-2 cm wide. Crumble the spooned-out cake in a separate bowl.

Filling ingredients:
- 500 ml of non-dairy whipping cream (sugar-free) + 200 ml for decorating – sweetened with 4.5 tablespoons of powdered fructose
- 150 g of grated diet chocolate
- 3-4 tablespoons of cooking rum
- 50 g of grated dark chocolate for decorating
Mix the crumbled cake with the whipped cream, rum,

sweetener, and grated chocolate.
Use this mass to fill in the hole in the center of the cake.
Form the filling into a dome shape, top with the remaining
whipped cream, and sprinkle with dark chocolate.
Cool the cake well.

On special occasions (holidays, birthdays) you can eat a slice
of this cake.

Diet coconut cake

This recipe is for a double-sized cake, since the cake can be
frozen and defrosted as needed.
You will need 3 plastic bowls (one extra large one).
First bowl – beaten egg whites:
Beat 10 egg whites with a pinch of salt until stiff. Add 3
tablespoons of powdered fructose to it.
Second bowl – liquid ingredients:
- 10 yolks
- 1 teaspoon of liquid artificial sweetener (Natreen)
- 5 dl of soy creamer
- 2 tablespoons of rum (or some other flavor, as desired)

Once you have beaten the egg whites, use the electric mixer
to beat the yolks in the second bowl until creamy, adding the
other liquid ingredients. Mix well.
Third bowl (largest) – dry ingredients:
- 12 rounded tablespoons of ground walnuts
- 12 rounded tablespoons of ground roasted hazelnuts
- 100 g of coconut flour
- 6 tablespoons of wholegrain barley flour
- 2 tablespoons of bitter cocoa powder
- 2 pouches of baking powder
- 5 tablespoons of fructose
Mix all the dry ingredients well with a wooden spoon.

Once the 3 bowls are ready, pour the liquid ingredients into the dry ingredients and mix well, then fold in the beaten egg whites.

Pour the dough into a large square pan (oven size) lined with parchment paper and place in an oven heated to 180°C. Bake for 20-30 minutes.

Once baked, make small holes on the top with a fork, and immediately top with 500 ml of soy milk (at room temperature).

Once the cake cools, top with chocolate frosting.

Chocolate frosting:

Melt 200 g of diet chocolate (in a double boiler or in a microwave oven) with hazelnuts and 100 g of organic margarine. Add 3 spoons of soy milk, mix everything well, and pour over the cake while still hot.

Cut the cake into 42 cubes (7 x 6 rows).

Three cubes of the cake can be a meal replacement, while one to two cubes can replace a snack when you feel like eating something sweet.

Diet crêpes
Batter ingredients:

- 3 eggs
- 1 teaspoon of powdered fructose
- 250 ml of soy creamer (one carton)
- 100 ml of soy milk
- 5 rounded tablespoons of ground roasted hazelnuts
- 3 tablespoons of wholegrain barley flour
- 1 level teaspoon of baking powder
- vanilla aroma
- grated peel from a large lemon

Preparation:
Mix the dry ingredients with a wooden spoon first (hazelnuts, fructose, barley flour and baking powder).
In another bowl, mix the liquid ingredients with a whisk (eggs, soy creamer, and milk).
Add the liquid ingredients to the dry ingredients and mix well.
Coat a small frying pan with butter and fry thicker crêpes (for easier flipping).

Fillings can include (as desired):
1. Diet marmalade or jam – 1 teaspoon per crêpe
2. Non-dairy whipped cream sweetened with fructose (if desired, add a small amount of bitter cocoa powder)
3. Melted diet chocolate
4. Fat-free fresh cheese, sweetened with fructose, with a flavor (concentrate) of your choice

Occasionally you can eat 3 crêpes a day, for breakfast or dinner, or along with coffee or tea.

About the Author

Dr. Tanya Skoro wrote this book for all victims of eating disorders who feel hopelessly stuck in the unbeatable trap of overeating. The book explains the mysterious causes leading to the onset of bulimia, as well as reasons which can maintain this disorder for years. It contains instructions for overcoming and abandoning the day-to-day suffering of bulimic patients, indicating which successful steps to take in order to attain health and peace of mind.

Dr. Tanya Skoro spent the last fifteen years treating eating disorders in her private medical office in Zagreb, Croatia.

She successfully applied her own Overcoming Bulimia Program in practice, and has recently published it in book form.

She lives in Istria now, writing books in an easy-to-read style, dealing with various eating disorders